Study of Nuclear and Alternative Energy Systems

SUPPORTING PAPER 7

ENERGY
CHOICES
IN A
DEMOCRATIC
SOCIETY

The Report of the
Consumption, Location, and Occupational Patterns Resource Group
Synthesis Panel
    of the
Committee on Nuclear and Alternative Energy Systems
National Research Council

NATIONAL ACADEMY OF SCIENCES
Washington, D.C.   1980

International Standard Book Number 0-309-03045-5

Library of Congress Catalog Card Number 80-81335

Available from:

Office of Publications
National Academy of Sciences
2101 Constitution Avenue, N.W.
Washington, D.C. 20418

Printed in the United States of America

To future generations--may they have choice.

The work for this study was carried out between the spring of 1976 and the summer of 1977 as a contribution to the Committee on Nuclear and Alternative Energy Systems (CONAES) of the National Research Council. The people who worked together on this project to imagine what life would be like under different energy conditions overcame disciplinary boundaries and faced the difficulties of convincing scientists and technologists of possibilities they had not imagined but which members of the general public were already living. The report was revised four times to incorporate reviewers' comments and new information that became available, but the basic message was the same throughout all four versions: energy is a social problem, not a technological one.

Since the time of completion of the last version in July 1977, events and information have continued to develop. As additional data have become available, some myths about energy have been dispelled, much to our pleasure, and in fact the conclusions of this study are continuing to be substantiated. It becomes clearer each day that the energy problem is a problem of value—that energy demand is part of the organization of preferences. It is not surprising, therefore, that there is controversy over what is possible. As an anthropologist I can afford to be expansive about the range of possibilities in terms of futures, for after all, anthropology is the study of many human possibilities; and the range of variety has been instructive indeed. Human societies are flexible over time.

Less adaptable and flexible, however, are the professionals. It became clear as we revised the report that we were trying to explain living habits in a way that could be understood in spite of the mind-sets of scientists of different professions participating in the CONAES study. Economists think that price determines everything. Physicists and chemists believe that progress means technological progress. Engineers believe that the language of numbers is somehow more precise than the language of words. While there are exceptions, most believe that what does not fit the mind-set is wrong or incompetent. Although I did try to accommodate to the standards that each professional group set for us, as chairperson of this resource group I was most interested in writing a report for the American taxpayer that would explain to him or her how the ideals of democracy and individual liberty can be either supported or sabotaged by the use and presence of specific technologies.

ACKNOWLEDGMENTS

Although a number of people contributed to each chapter, a few individuals were mainly responsible for conceiving and executing each chapter. Laura Nader wrote the foreword and the introductory and final chapters; Robert Olson wrote Chapter 2. Laura Nader and Stephen Beckerman developed the materials for Chapter 3. Paul Craig contributed Chapter 4. Peter Benenson was the principal author of Chapter 5; he was aided by Lee Schipper and David Pilati. Laura Nader, Cathie Jane Witty, and Lee Schipper are primarily responsible for Chapter 6. The brief concluding remarks in Chapter 7 are an anthropological reminder that experts are playing a central role in fashioning the "possible" and the "impossible" in energy planning. Overall responsibility for the editing, organizing, and review was that of the chairperson, who, in the tradition of such Academy studies, performed this task without remuneration from the Academy or, unlike their counterparts in corporations, release time from the University of California. The unsigned preface was written by the Academy staff.

We wish to thank the many who also gave of their advice, knowledge, and skill in the process of formulating this document. Robert L. Olson, W. W. Harman, Mary Foster, Clarence Glacken, Nelson Graburn, Steve Beckerman, Otis Dudley Duncan, Lester Lave, Norman Milleron, Elizabeth Colson, and John Holdren, among others, contributed in writing and critical appraisal. In particular, we thank Otis Dudley Duncan, a member of CONAES until he resigned, for his useful advice and for the model he is of a scientist with integrity and sensitivity to the qualitative questions. Belinda Johns contributed her skills and organizational abilities. Grace Buzaljko, Robert Cantwell, and others contributed to the editing process. Many people supported us in collating, looking up references, and the myriad of tasks necessary to such a project: Liz Goldstein, Dorothy Koenig, Kathleen Bradley, Pat Brooks, Lane Hirabayashi, and Cathy Rich. In addition, I personally wish to thank the Woodrow Wilson International Center for Scholars in Washington, D.C. for its support, in 1979-80, during the very final stages of this manuscript.

Laura Nader
Washington, D.C.
March 1980

In June, 1975, the National Research Council (NRC) undertook a comprehensive study of the nation's prospective energy economy during the period 1985-2010, with special attention to the role of nuclear power among the alternative energy systems. The goal of the study is to assist the American people and government in formulating energy policy.

The Governing Board of the National Research Council appointed an NRC-wide Committee on Nuclear and Alternative Energy Systems (CONAES) to conduct the study. CONAES consists of 15 members drawn from diverse disciplines and backgrounds. The committee developed a three-tiered functional structure for the study. The first tier is CONAES itself. The ultimate findings, judgments, and conclusions of the study will be embodied in its final report.

To provide scientific and engineering data and analyses, a second tier of four panels was formed to examine (1) energy demand and conservation, (2) energy supply and delivery systems, (3) risks and impacts of energy supply and use, and (4) syntheses of diverse models of future energy economies, respectively. Each panel, in turn, established a number of resource groups--22 in all--as the third tier, to address in detail an array of more particular matters, such as buildings and transportation systems, solar energy, breeder reactors, coal technologies, health and environmental implications, and alternative consumption patterns and economic models. In all, more than 200 informed individuals served on or contributed to the work of the panels and resource groups.

The National Research Council customarily publishes only the final reports of its committees--and then only after the report has been reviewed by a group other than its authors according to procedures approved by a Report Review Committee consisting of members of the National Academy of Sciences, the National Academy of Engineering, and the Institute of Medicine. However, because such a large volume of information and analyses was assembled for consideration by the committee, and because of the diversity and scope of that information and the accompanying judgments, the panel reports and approximately 10 reports by the resource groups are being published as supporting papers. Each of these has been considered by CONAES but has not undergone the critical review procedure normal to the NRC. The report of the Consumption, Location,

and Occupational Patterns Resource Group has, however, been subjected to
a thorough and expert peer review for accuracy, consistency, and
clarity.

It must be recognized that some conclusions of the panel and
resource group report may be at variance with the conclusions of the
CONAES report. The findings reported in these documents are those of
their authors and are not necessarily endorsed by CONAES or the National
Research Council.

This report covers the work of the Consumption, Location and
Occupational Patterns Resource Group of the Synthesis Panel, done for
the most part in 1977-1978. It is published, with the other supporting
papers to enrich the general understanding of the intricate and wide-
ranging implications of energy policy in the coming decades and to
acquaint the reader with the variety and complexity of the material
with which CONAES has had to deal.

CONSUMPTION, LOCATION, AND OCCUPATIONAL

PATTERNS RESOURCE GROUP

LAURA NADER (Chairperson), Professor, Department of Anthropology,
University of California at Berkeley

PETER BENENSON, Economist, University of California, Lawrence Berkeley
Laboratory

NORMAN BRADBURN, Chairman, Department of Behavioral Sciences, University
of Chicago

CLARK BULLARD, Research Assistant Professor, Center for Advanced
Computation, University of Illinois at Urbana

PAUL CRAIG, Department of Applied Science, University of California at
Davis

DAVID PILATI, Research Assistant Professor, Center for Advanced
Computation, University of Illinois at Urbana

LEE SCHIPPER, Lawrence Berkeley Laboratory, University of California at
Berkeley

CATHIE J. WITTY, Program in Medical Anthropology, University of
California, San Francisco

SYNTHESIS PANEL

LESTER B. LAVE (Chairman), Senior Fellow, Brookings Institution

RICHARD E. BALZHISER, Director, Fossil Fuel and Advanced Systems
Division, Electric Power Research Institute

DAVID COHEN, President, Common Cause

CHARLES O. JONES, Maurice Falk Professor of Politics, Department
of Political Science, University of Pittsburgh

TJALLING C. KOOPMANS, Alfred Cowles Professor of Economics, Cowles
Foundation for Research in Economics, Yale University

LAURA NADER, Professor, Department of Anthropology, University of
California at Berkeley

WILLIAM D. NORDHAUS, John Musser Professor of Economics, Cowles
Foundation for Research in Economics, Yale University

SAM H. SCHURR, Senior Fellow and Co-Director, Energy and Materials
Division, Resources for the Future, Inc.

JON M. VEIGEL, Director of Research and Development, Energy Resources,
Conservation and Development Commission, State of California

DAVID O. WOOD, Program Director, Energy Economics and Management
Division, Energy Laboratory, Massachusetts Institute of Technology

---

BRIAN CRISSEY, Staff Officer

JAMES E. JUST, Consultant

x

COMMITTEE ON NUCLEAR AND ALTERNATIVE ENERGY SYSTEMS

HARVEY BROOKS (Co-Chairman), Benjamin Peirce Professor of Technology
    and Public Policy, Aiken Computation Laboratory, Harvard University

EDWARD L. GINZTON (Co-Chairman), Chairman of the Board, Varian Associates

KENNETH E. BOULDING, Distinguished Professor of Economics, Institute of
    Behavioral Science, University of Colorado

ROBERT H. CANNON, JR., Chairman, Division of Engineering and Applied
    Science, California Institute of Technology

EDWARD J. GORNOWSKI, Executive Vice President, Exxon Research and
    Engineering Company

JOHN P. HOLDREN, Professor, Energy and Resources Program, University of
    California at Berkeley

HENDRIK S. HOUTHAKKER, Henry Lee Professor of Economics, Department of
    Economics, Harvard University

HENRY I. KOHN, Professor, Radiation Biology, Shields Warren Radiation
    Laboratory

STANLEY J. LEWAND, Vice President, Public Utilities Division, The Chase
    Manhattan Bank

LUDWIG F. LISCHER, Vice President of Engineering, Commonwealth Edison
    Company

JOHN C. NEESS, Professor of Zoology, University of Wisconsin

DAVID ROSE, Professor, Nuclear Engineering, Massachusetts Institute of
   Technology

DAVID SIVE, Attorney at Law, Winer, Neuberger and Sive

BERNARD I. SPINRAD, Professor, Nuclear Engineering, Radiation Center,
   Oregon State University

JACK M. HOLLANDER, Study Director

JOHN O. BERGA, Deputy Study Director

CONTENTS

TABLES

1 INTRODUCTION

One major characteristic of the twentieth century is a growing dependence of individuals and groups on large institutions. Over the past
40 years both individual and group self-reliance have dramatically
decreased. Wage labor and specialization is the overwhelming pattern
and dependency the theme. With increased dependence have come increased
government planning, increased reliance on expertise, and an increasingly disunited society with different segments operating as strangers
to one another.

The problems of our world today have a seamless quality about them.
Such problems do not recognize the narrow confines of expertise of professional managers. Energy is a social, not a technological, issue.
Yet in so many discussions of the factual basis of energy the cultural
and social contexts tend to be left implicit. The major choices in
energy paths are being made in the context of different and often conflicting perceptions and beliefs. For example, one set of beliefs
would see the energy problem as one of developing new supplies to meet
the expanding energy needs; another might see the problem as one of
reducing energy appetites, and yet another belief system might perceive
the energy problem as a choice between hazardous, centralized systems
and decentralized systems that had less hazardous potential. The differing ideologies are associated not only with different expert advice,
but also with differing organizations of expert knowledge.

The authors of this study believe that most Americans are uncertain
about the consequences for all of us of differing plans for the future
in energy. In order that citizens be better informed, and that the
nation not foreclose any options that, decades from now, we may wish we
had chosen, the authors prepared this report to provide some pictures
of the future that represent alternatives to those of the traditional
industrial and technological views.

It is good to keep in mind while reading this report that we write about the United States and not the world, but that we write also about a specific type of culture and society. The United States is but a part of an industrial civilization founded on the principle of ever-expanding consumption. We measure our standard of living largely in terms of material consumption and by means of numbers. Modern cultures, such as that of the United States, outgrow local boundaries and consume greater and greater amounts of the world's resources, leaving less for future generations. Sometimes such habits have caused major discontinuities even in preindustrial civilizations: witness the Mediterranean basin when Rome denuded it of wood (Rostovstev, 1957) or the many societies that suffered from soil erosion because of destructive agricultural practices. Resources that could have been renewed were used thoughtlessly and so ceased to yield wood, food, and other desired products. The challenge today is to explore alternatives that are consistent with long-run ecological success, in drawing on renewable resources only.

What are the full social benefits, costs, and risks of a national shift toward reduced total energy consumption and maximum reliance on renewable energy sources? What will it mean to the way Americans live in the year 2010 to reduce the amount of energy we use?

We examine these questions by dividing this report into three sections. First, we explore pictures of our society in the year 2010 as imagined by different groups of futurists, sorting out their predictions in terms of certain significant factors (Chapter 2). Next, we examine the two most plausible sources of long-term energy supply--the breeder reactor (Chapter 3) and solar energy (Chapter 4)--and the consequences for the year 2010 of both choices. Next, we concentrate on two portrayals of the year 2010, in both of which the United States is assumed to curtail its demand for energy. These portrayals are disciplined exercises, not descriptions of utopian societies. One is a 72-quad[a] society (Chapter 5); the other is a 53-quad society (Chapter 6). (For purposes of comparison, the United States used 71.2 quads in 1975; and the typical 1000-megawatt--1-gigawatt--power plant has an annual output of 0.1 quad or less.) Our final chapter raises the question of who ought to decide which energy policy will take us to the kind of society we wish to have by the year 2010.

THE FUTURISTS

Taken together, and despite their profound differences, many futurists make a case that energy policy is a key area of social decision making for this generation because energy policy permeates the whole pattern of culture. It is critically important, therefore, that major energy-policy decisions are not made solely on the basis of political expediency,

---

[a]Quad is a term that appears repeatedly in these pages. It is the customary abbreviation for one quadrillion (1,000,000,000,000,000) British thermal units (Btu's).

bureaucratic self-interest, narrow and specialized perspectives, or short-term profit considerations at the expense of future generations.

The very meaning of progress is at issue. Does increased income produce increased satisfaction? Is further urbanization desirable, or would it be better to live a more rural life? At what pace do we want to live? What are the gains and losses in the trend away from self-employment toward employment in large organizations? Is increasing leisure progress, or do we need to reexamine the relationship of leisure and work? Is there a proper human scale for our institutions? Do we want to expand our use of initiatory democracy? How much importance should be given to the renewal of strong local community ties? How vulnerable to sabotage and terrorism are we willing to be? How much weight should we give to international and intergenerational equity? By relating energy consumption to questions like these, the futurists make it dramatically clear that the major energy-policy choices before us are not so much technical decisions as moral choices, choices about how we want to live, for which technical expertise gives no special guidance or competence. These choices deserve the most thorough consideration and the widest possible participation by the members of a society.

The futurists have clearly moved beyond the sterile debate between the advocates of growth and the advocates of no growth. Attention to the physical and biological outer limits of growth is broadening to consider as well the impact of different kinds and rates of growth on the quality of life. To substitute a dogma of no growth for the dogma of materialism would be to substitute one emptiness for another. We must leave behind the purely quantitative concepts of energy and economic growth and insist on the primacy of qualitative ideas.

The futurist literature, taken as a whole, sets out a new attitude toward the growth debate that could profitably be adopted. Because energy growth cannot continue indefinitely, we now ask (Nader and Beckerman, 1978) when energy growth will have to be slowed or stopped, and at what level. Since we are uncertain about many of the factors that would cause us to limit energy use, what is a prudent course of action now? Are there changes in technology and lifestyle that can enhance the quality of life while lowering the level of energy consumption? How can necessary or desirable changes best be made? Facing the issues squarely and attempting to examine the implications of the alternatives open to us will help to prevent the extreme stereotyping and polarization that frustrates communication, increases rigidity, and blocks mutual understanding.

SOURCES OF ENERGY SUPPLY

Our discussions of energy supply—of solar energy and nuclear breeder reactors, for example—focus on how different value systems might or might not lead to reliance on renewable resources. The United States is involved in an extensive but as yet not clearly focused debate on the future of the national energy system. The bulk of the discussion thus far has concentrated on the economics of such massive new technologies as coal gasification and nuclear power. A variety of considerations, such as a national decision to move toward renewable resources, could change this emphasis.

Many of the issues that we raise in our analysis of the breeder reactor, such as proliferation of nuclear weapons, catastrophic reactor accidents, long-term safeguarding of nuclear waste, and infringement of liberties as a result of safeguard procedures, also apply to nonbreeding reactors. Nevertheless, we limit our discussion to breeder systems[a] because, compared with the short life span of nonbreeding nuclear technology, the long lives of both breeder and solar systems offer the prospect of energy into the indefinite future.

In spite of the fact that there has been abundant research in the nuclear field since 1945, relatively little has been concerned with the impact of this technology on human affairs. The bulk of the discussion has concentrated on technical issues like the adequacy of the emergency core-cooling systems in light-water reactors, and not on the impact of nuclear energy on society and government. Even within this concentration on technology there are many unanswered questions of overwhelming importance, such as the problems of handling nuclear waste and decommissioning old reactors. But if we are to develop a coherent energy policy, both technical and social questions must be answered. For example, large-scale bureaucratic centralization is a likely result of a national breeder system (Lovins, 1976). Necessary safeguards may (some would argue already do) drastically reduce civil rights, with a general increase in numbers and power of police (Ayres, 1975). To our knowledge there are now no dossiers on individuals who are antisolar, or anticonservation, but there is evidence that dossiers exist on antinuclear advocates.[b]

---

[a] It may come as a surprise to some that nonbreeding reactors have a short life span of about 35 years and as a technology can be useful only while uranium is available (predicted to be 50 years or less).

[b] Research on civil rights aspects of technologies needs to be encouraged. Specifically on the cited points there is the following documentation:

The New York Times (1974) has reported that the Texas state police compiled dossiers generated by noncriminal investigation. Specifically, it cited the dossier on a former marine, then a Continental Airlines pilot in Dallas, who was the leader of a local group opposing nuclear plants.

The Washington Post (Edwards, 1975) reported that the Virginia Electric and Power Company (VEPCO) in January 1975 asked a representative in the state legislature to submit a bill that would give VEPCO authority to establish its own police force with power to arrest anywhere in the state and to gain access to confidential citizen records. The bill was subsequently withdrawn when some citizens protested.

In July, 1976 a joint Energy Research and Development Administration-Nuclear Regulatory Commission task force recommended full security checks on selected employees of facilities handling nuclear material (U.S. Nuclear Regulatory, 1976).

Solar energy offers the technical potential for meeting a large proportion of the nation's energy needs. The time required to phase in a solar-based system will depend on the vigor of the undertaking, the strength of national commitment, and the degree to which solar-energy systems prove economical compared with other new systems. Strong institutional factors make exploitation of solar energy difficult and slow: competing interests, a scarcity of experts in the field, and the possibility that solar-energy systems do not easily lend themselves to monopoly.

The relative advantages and disadvantages of the breeder reactor and solar energy depend crucially on nonmarket costs and benefits, often unquantifiable, which may be more important than the factors that can be easily quantified. They must be considered explicitly and carefully in any comparison of these technologies (Holdren, 1976).

ALTERNATIVE SOCIETIES

The first society that we describe was developed to explore the use of energy in a future society that looks very much like today's, without major changes in attitudes but with significant improvements in amenities, with improvements roughly consistent with those that have occurred in recent decades, and with prudent energy use as well. In the second instance, we explore a society in which attitudes toward resources have changed significantly, work has been decentralized, and thrift and self-reliance are valued; this society is less vulnerable to terrorism and violence than the first, and better supplied with the amenities of life. The energy consumption levels associated with these two societies are 72 and 53 quads, respectively.

Even with growth in population and per-capita gross national product (GNP), the total energy consumption in the first society is approximately the same in 2010 as it is today. Moreover, this level of consumption could be attained without significant reorganization of life, work, or transportation. It is important to note that the behavioral and technological changes that lead to energy saving do not restrict production of goods and services. Instead, they imply simply more efficient production and use of goods and services. The 72-quad high-energy-productivity society we have developed embodies significant conservation

---

After the death of Karen Silkwood in November, 1974, the Kerr-McGee Nuclear Facility conducted lie detector tests for all employees at its plutonium plant. The questions asked were the following: "Are you a member of the union?" "Do you take or use narcotics?" "Did you ever talk to Karen Silkwood?" "Have you ever done anything detrimental to Kerr-McGee?" "Have you talked to the press or media?" Workers who refused to take the test or who did not pass the test were either fired or demoted. This was reported before the House Committee on Small Business (U.S. Congress, 1976).

The Center for Science in the Public Interest (Washington, D.C.) is exploring the kinds of surveillance techniques that are being used in relation to vulnerable technologies.

of energy, achieved by a variety of mechanisms ranging from economic policy to regulations, education, market signals, and research and development.

The second society that we describe is a high-technology, low-energy consumption society. This 53-quad society explores the potential for energy reduction associated with changes in attitudes. The primary thrust of the analysis is toward qualitative shifts. The people in this society do not attempt to turn back the clock, but they do try to use technology in ways that improve the quality of life. Advanced technology appears at many points: solar energy, advanced automobiles, magnetically levitated trains, microprocessor building and process control systems, extensive use of cogeneration, and so on.

We emphasize longevity of products. Boulding (1949-1950) demonstrated that it is stocks of goods that contribute to human well-being, while flows contribute to GNP. This shift in emphasis leads to processes intended to minimize resource consumption over time. The shift in cultural attitudes embodied in the 53-quad society will necessitate the development by economists and other social scientists of new measures of the progress of society. These new attitudes define a society that attempts to preserve stocks and to minimize resource flow.

The scale of this 53-quad society reflects the needs of a participatory democracy. The trends toward tightly meshed technological systems characteristic of the 1970's are reversed in the 53-quad society, increasing the likelihood that most of the system can survive if a part of it is severely damaged. The stability of a technological system depends on the types of external perturbation that occur and on the types of redundancy built in.

Overall, the new attitudes in society result from major changes in the most important factors affecting gross energy demand. Efficiency increases significantly, because of large price increases and conservation programs. There is no per-capita growth in GNP, as the GNP becomes a less useful measure of well-being. Attitudes toward transportation, throw-away products, and space conditioning change; attitudes toward other important aspects of life not usually discussed in connection with energy, such as quality of interpersonal relations and participation in processes that determine the quality and direction of everyday affairs, change as well.

There are several important lessons to be learned from this second society. There are many, although not limitless, ways to use 53 quads or any other amount of energy; individual lives vary in their energy use regardless of the energy available. Certain supply technologies are less intrusive than others. Change from the grass roots, combined with planned change by government, will have effects and results different from those imposed by directives from the top.

Life has changed since the turn of the century and will change as we move into the next century, no matter what our energy policy may be. There is no basis for the belief that the continued growth of our present technology would not effect a dramatic change in lifestyle. Such growth has changed and will continue to change the fabric of U.S. and world society, and lifestyles will change with or without technology.

Consideration of low-energy, high-technology scenarios expands the range of choice and may increase the time within which we can plan for the age after fossil fuels.

IDEOLOGY, EXPERTISE, AND THE PUBLIC

Energy research dealing with human factors, social and cultural, has received remarkably little attention to date. We know something about the technology of energy, but much less about the agents: the experts, the interest groups, the public. Expert actors in the energy picture often contribute to the public's confusion about energy issues, for expertise is often accompanied by an isolation from the public to be served, which leads to distorted or unrealistic views of what the problem is and what the public does or does not want. There should be more open debate and discussion.

We need to understand something about the social organization of energy experts. Who are they? What is their rank? Do nuclear physicists and engineers, for instance, dominate the late-coming biologists, health physicists, and social scientists? What is the relationship between the experts who estimate the probabilities of harmful events and those who assess their consequences?

Furthermore, for both the societies described we need to know more about implementation mechanisms. For example, we need to know about the comparative advantages of market mechanisms, voluntary means, and government measures, such as mandatory efficiency standards for buildings, automobiles and appliances. We also need to know how to teach people to use resources well (Callenbach, 1972).

The forms of cities are significant determinants of energy use. There is little information about the relationship between the variety of city forms and total energy use. This should be analyzed, along with the evolution of cities and of transportation patterns associated with alternative governmental policies.

Our understanding of the vulnerability of low- and high-energy living is incomplete. Under what conditions does a low- or high-energy-use scenario increase our vulnerability to technical failure? What makes us vulnerable? Is the energy system constructed so that a failure of one part leads to public rejection of the whole concept? If there is a catastrophe, what is the recovery period--years or generations?

We need to know something about barriers to certain kinds of research. Conventional economic theory has it that people's desires operate through the market to create profit for technological developments that meet these desires. In the United States today most research and development is initially funded outside the market, so that the values of most people, which would be reflected in a perfect market, are not the motivating force. Research and development allocation is made by a small group of scientists and civil servants in government agencies that may be insulated from the people.

The lesson in this report is simple. The future offers a broad and rich range of choices; what seems possible at present depends on our bias toward high- or low-energy use. The human component must be recognized as the primary factor in the success or failure of technologies--a factor that has never been free of error. Efficient problem solving requires cooperation among the public, their government, and the business community.

When the Committee on Nuclear and Alternative Energy Systems was established, it was assumed that energy prices would increase slowly, corresponding to an approximate doubling by 2010. In fact, events of the last year have shown that 2010 has arrived. Many of the technologies that looked as if they would be economical by the turn of the century are economical today, and the future described in this report, which looked extreme when it was first written, makes rational social and economic sense today. If anything, our energy demand estimates seem high. The reversal has been profound.

It is interesting, in terms of project sociology, that the shift projected in our report was viewed as beyond the pale when it was first presented. The events of the last few years have made a report that was thought to be extremely controversial look not only plausible but even conservative.

As we said in earlier versions of this study, predictions are problematic. Such possibilities as the Iranian revolution and the Three Mile Island accident are not built into our thinking about the future.

REFERENCES

Ayres, R. W. 1975. Policing Plutonium: The Civil Liberties Fallout.
Harvard Civil Rights-Civil Liberties Law Review 10(2):369-443.

Boulding, K. 1949-1950. Income or Welfare. Review of Economic
Studies 17(2):77-86.

Callenbach, E. 1972. Living Poor with Style. New York: Bantam
Books.

Edwards, P. G. 1975. Bill to Allow Virginia Utilities to Name Own
Police Sought. Washington Post, January 18, p. E3.

Holdren, J. 1976. Technology, Environment, and Well-being--Some
Critical Choices. In Growth in America, ed. C. L. Cooper.
Westport, Conn.: Greenwood Press.

Lovins, A. 1976. Energy Strategy: The Road Not Taken. Foreign
Affairs 55(1):65-96.

Nader, R., and S. Beckerman. 1978. Energy as It Relates to the
Quality and Style of Life. Annual Review of Energy, ed. Jack M.
Hollander, 2d ed. 3:1-28. Palo Alto, Calif.: Annual Reviews.

New York Times. 1974. Texas Agency Destroys Disputed Files. New
York Times, August 25, p. 38.

Rostovstev, M. I. 1957. Social and Economic History of the Roman
Empire, 2d ed. Oxford, England: Clarendon Press.

U.S. Congress. 1976. Problems in the Accounting for a Safeguarding
of Special Nuclear Materials. Testimony by Anthony Mazzocchi and
Steven Wodka. Hearings before the Subcommittee on Energy and
Environment of the Committee on Small Business, April 26, May 7, 20.
94th Cong., 2d sess. Washington, D.C.: U.S. Government Printing
Office.

U.S. Nuclear Regulatory Commission and U.S. Energy Research and
Development Administration. 1976. Joint ERDA-NRC Task Force on
Safeguards, Final Report. Springfield, Va.: National Technical
Information Service (ERDA-77-34).

2 CONTRAST OF FOUR ALTERNATIVE FUTURES

IN TWELVE DIMENSIONS

As we noted in Chapter 1, several professional futurists and future-
oriented social critics have examined the relationship between energy
consumption and lifestyle. Their long-run perspectives and their emphasis on broad cultural changes can help to expand the intellectual framework for making energy policy.

This chapter contrasts four groups of futurists according to their
predictions about 12 different dimensions of life in the future. We
have termed these groups "Superindustrial" (Kahn and Bruce-Briggs, 1972;
Kahn, Brown, and Martel, 1976), "Plenitude" (Armstrong and Harman, 1975;
Harman, 1976), "Small Is Beautiful" (Callenbach, 1975; Goodman and
Goodman, 1960; Schumacher, 1973), and "Minimum Feasible" (Illich, 1973,
1974; Raskin, 1973). From each group it is possible to learn something
about the wider context and consequences of energy use.

NATURAL ENVIRONMENT

Superindustrial: Rapid energy growth can provide wealth, the recycling,
the cleaner industrial processes, and the improved pollution control
necessary for protecting the environment. Moderate pollution is inevitable and worth the benefits of which it is a cost.

Plenitude: The most energy-intensive nations are approaching a
new scarcity, which includes a reduction in the resilience and waste-
absorbing capacity of the natural environment. As a result, energy
growth might occur more selectively and slowly. Achieving energy frugality and improving the natural environment could be complementary
parts of an inspiring "central project" for America.

Small is Beautiful: We do not know how close the many smaller imbalances that we have induced in the natural environment have come to be more generalized, and so the greatest caution is required. A safe course is to set a global example by making a transition to a less energy-intensive lifestyle that would without question be environmentally sound if adopted by all humanity. The attainment of stable-state life systems should become the fundamental goal of politics, and even a religious objective.

Minimum Feasible: Calories are both biologically and socially healthful only as long as they stay within the narrow range that separates enough from too much. The United States has long since exceeded the environmentally optimal range of energy use; as a result the environment must be increasingly "protected," at the cost of increased social control, large centralized government, and technocracy.

SETTLEMENT PATTERNS

Superindustrial: There will be an increasing movement to urban and suburban as opposed to rural areas; urban sprawls will grow as peak densities decrease in metropolitan areas. In the twenty-first century there will be growth of "urban regions" as megalopolises overlap and merge.

Plenitude: The population will be predominantly urbanized, but there will be a gradual decentralization, with new designs in transportation networks, land use, and waste disposal. A larger percentage of the population will be engaged in agriculture on smaller, more labor-intensive farms. Manufacturing will be more widely dispersed to produce goods in closer proximity to raw materials and to users. Joint federal and private enterprises will experiment with small-scale future frontier cities designed to test and exhibit energy-frugal physical designs, technologies, lifestyles, and policies.

Small Is Beautiful: The point at which large size detracts more than it adds to a city is probably reached when there are half a million inhabitants. Cities of this size could be the great cities of a decentralized agro-industrial settlement pattern, which would intentionally integrate rural and urban life to bring people close to nature, permit children to be reared in natural environments, and recycle wastes efficiently. Relatively self-contained regions composed of mini-cities of 9,000-10,000 people, each part of a necklace of towns linked by rapid transit, could eventually contain most of the population.

Minimum Feasible: Highly decentralized settlements could exist in a social context of self-sufficient, small-scale community life, much like Gandhi's vision of a global society composed of villages, but based on greater knowledge.

OCCUPATIONS

Superindustrial: Energy and economic growth will continue at a high level to generate full employment. There will be decreasing employment in primary economic activities (agriculture, mining, fishing, forestry) and secondary economic activities (construction, manufacturing), and more employment in tertiary services (transportation, finance, management, government) and in quaternary services (learning, communications, services to services). The trend from self-employment to a nation of employees in large, impersonal organizations will continue.

Plenitude: There must be a profound shift in the very conception of what work is; in a technologically advanced society, employment exists primarily for self-development and only secondarily for production itself, which can be handled with ease. The right to full and valued participation is a new fundamental political right, but the problem of "superflous" people grows more serious as society becomes more highly industrialized, substituting greater and greater energy consumption for human labor. True unemployment--among women who desire jobs, the young and elderly who are squeezed out of the job market, the despairing who no longer seek work, people who are institutionalized--ranged between 25 and 35 percent of the potential work force in 1976, and this problem will grow worse as economic growth slows. There will be a need for selective increases in labor intensity to increase employment in various primary and secondary economic activities, such as farming, fishing, forestry, and craftsmanship. There will also be a need to provide both temporary and longer term support for people who have demonstrated the ability to hold structured jobs but who want to carry out projects of manifest social value, such as study and research, providing learning opportunities for others, preserving and beautifying the environment, carrying out social experiments, assisting the handicapped, creating in the arts, and providing companionship for the aged. Such provision would open jobs for people who desire structured jobs to attain a higher standard of living and to grow in self-management ability. The need for public works projects and public service employment will continue.

Small Is Beautiful: The function of work is threefold: to allow people to use and develop their abilities, to enable them to overcome self-centeredness by joining in common tasks, and to bring forth the goods and services needed for existence. Thus it is irrational to replace labor with energy at the price of failing to achieve full employment for all who need it, and it is wrong to organize work so that it becomes meaningless, boring, stultifying, or nerve-racking. Energy-intensive technology has reduced the amount of time spent on production in its most elementary sense to about 3.5 percent of total social time. This should be increased to about 20 percent. Productive work should be consciously designed on psychological and moral grounds so that it can be a satisfying way of life. We must reverse the trend from self-employment to employment in impersonal, bureaucratic organizations, and we must also reduce the trend toward the separation of home and work environments and the isolation of work from education.

Minimum Feasible: Employment must be based on a complete restructuring of industrial society away from "manipulative" institutions and tools, which by their very nature restrict to a very few the liberty to use them in an autonomous way. Occupations based on "convivial" tools and institutions will usually be part of institutions that are small

in scale and use little energy, because the growth of institutions and
tools beyond a certain point tends to increase regimentation, dependence,
and exploitation.

LEISURE

Superindustrial: Leisure will increase as labor productivity continues
to rise, and it may result in boredom and bizarre behavior. An increasingly aristocratic and formal way of life may arise, with increasing
tourism, ritualistic activities, arts, entertaining, sports and competitive games, TV watching, and quests for broadening experiences, adven-
ture, excitement, and amusement. People would be freed for many
activities more enjoyable and worthwhile than work.

Plenitude: Better education and greater material wealth are bring-
ing a shift in emphasis from a materially extravagant society, bereft of
a sense of direction, toward a materially frugal, human growth society
in which realizing the fullest human potential of each person is the
central project of American life. Only in the context of an inspiring
sense of individual and cultural purpose can leisure be increased significantly without bad psychological and social effects.

Small Is Beautiful: We give lip service to the traditional virtues
of hard work, but at the same time our intellectual leaders treat (other
people's) work as nothing but a necessary evil to be abolished and
replaced as quickly as possible by a life of automated leisure. This
intellectual confusion about the relationship between leisure and work
exacts a high price, of which worker motivation is just a small part.
To strive for more and more leisure as an alternative to work is to
misunderstand completely one of the basic truths of human experience--
that work and leisure are part of the same living process and cannot be
separated without destroying the joy of both. Regulation of work time
and separation of work from the home environment are signs that work is
not a way of life. When work is a way of life, then work is itself
leisurely, playful, creative, and satisfying. Greater leisure is psy-
chologically wholesome only when leisure is not an escape from unful-
filling work.

Minimum Feasible: The harried leisure class in super-consumption
societies becomes time-poor as it becomes goods-rich. Time-intensive
activities, such as friendship, reflection, meditation, and care for the
aged and children, are sacrificed in favor of commodity-intensive activities, which are constantly promoted by massive advertising that appeals
to subconscious fears and sexual interests. Approximately 250 hunting
and gathering bands have survived into the twentieth century. Many
students of these cultures argue that such "primitive" peoples have more
leisure time, far deeper interpersonal relationships, and a richer folk
culture than people in modern civilization. (See, for example, Turnbull,
1961.) We need to deemphasize commodity-intensive activities radically
and to use energy mainly to relieve the rigor of the most backbreaking
and boring tasks.

PERSONAL POSSESSIONS

Superindustrial: By 2025, the United States GNP per capita will be
$20,000. The problem of poverty will be solved, and most misery will
derive from the anxieties and ambiguities of wealth and luxury, not from
lack of possessions. There will be a growing aristocratic taste for
luxuries: the finest automobiles, country homes, exotic imported foods
and products, and expensive works of art.

Plenitude: Plenitude allows for extravagant expenditures to satisfy
major needs, but many people may deliberately choose a life of voluntary
simplicity in which competitive consumption will not be used to establish
identity distinctions. The "freedom" of frugality (freedom from the need
to spend time earning a large income, the need to conform to a particular
fashion, the need to "keep up with the Joneses," etc.) could be used to
explore largely nonmaterial dimensions of human growth such as wide
learning, bodily fitness and health, full human development and child-
rearing, personal honesty and responsibility in group relationships, and
meditative and other practices for consciousness change and new "powers
of mind."

Small Is Beautiful: There is ultimately no resolution of our energy,
environmental, and social problems as long as there is no idea of "enough"
being good and "more than enough" being bad. To assume that more consumption is always better is to confuse means and ends: since consumption is
only a means to human well-being, the intelligent aim should be to obtain
the maximum of well-being with the minimum of consumption. The ideal of
good, modest, comfortable living ought to replace the ideal of affluence.
Then people would desire relatively few possessions and value functional-
ity, durability, and easy repair, and yet take delight in fine tools and
in simple possessions such as clothing, musical instruments, and furniture of handmade quality and artistry. Some possessions could be owned
in common and shared by family and neighborhood groups.

Minimum Feasible: In our cultural chauvinism, we take our rampant
materialism so much for granted that it comes as a surprise to learn--if
we will even accept the fact--that there are many cultures with a radically different emphasis. The Ontong Javanese, for example, have no
word in their language for personal poverty, since possessions are shared
within kinship groups. Although their standard of living is simple and
has remained static for centuries, it would never occur to them that they
are unhappy for lack of possessions. They consider a person poor not
when he lacks possessions, but when he lacks intimate friends, compatible
working partners, or close family relationships. This kind of psychic
poverty is now a major affliction of superconsumption societies.

INSTITUTIONAL SCALE

Superindustrial: The future will see a decreased dependence on family
or communal institutions, high mobility with a loss of a sense of residential community, and more time spent in impersonal organizations and
institutions. The Federal government will continue to increase its

importance in relation to state and local governments; multinational corporations will continue to grow rapidly; nation states and multinational corporations will increasingly become central social institutions.

Plenitude: Guidance by the federal government is crucial for establishing a learning and planning society that could then rearrange the society's institutional scale. In a downward direction, moderate decentralization of settlement patterns, industry, and agriculture would create smaller and less complex living and working environments that are more comprehensible, more approachable, and more amenable to direction and control at the local level. Family and community would increase in importance. In an upward direction, new covenants and management structures would provide increasing transnational coordination: a world food stockpile and distribution system, a world nuclear peace-keeping covenant, a world population covenant, an ocean management authority, multinational development boards, and multinational antitrust agreements (because multinational corporations will increase in importance).

Small Is Beautiful: Large-scale organization is here to stay. What we need is not _either_ large-scale _or_ small-scale organization but a proper mix of both. Today, however, we suffer from an almost universal ideology of gigantism accepted by the political right wing, left wing, and middle of the road. It is therefore necessary to insist on the virtue of smallness where it can be applied.

Minimum Feasible: If we could examine the relationship between institutional scale and the satisfactoriness of life without vested interest or fear, we would see that our institutions are not expressive of people's real values. Our society has completely lost its human scale. Society should be organized on the basis of voluntary cooperation of relatively autonomous, self-determining, small-scale communities. But communities cannot be autonomous and self-determining if they are addicted to massive amounts of outside energy.

DISPERSION OF DECISION-MAKING POWER

Superindustrial: There will be continued centralization and concentration of economic power in multinational corporations and of political power in the federal government; a continued trend toward interchangeability of high-level personnel between business and government; a continued trend toward increasing military capability and a larger military-industrial complex; and continued rise of elites and specialists. This is the way the world seems to be going in the long run, like it or not. The level of management required is not remarkably high: the systematic internalization of relevant external costs and the normal use of price and other market mechanisms can deal with most issues.

Plentitude: A difficult period of transition to a more frugal society is anticipated, with a great danger of the establishment of an authoritarian government to maintain stability. The transition can be smoothed, and an authoritarian concentration of power checked, by a voluntary and collective redirection of the whole society, with widespread understanding of the need for new social goals and willingness to make individual decisions in accordance with the changing overall pattern of social values. In the transition period, new management structures need to be designed for effectively employing widespread citizen participation at local, regional, national, and global levels. The resulting society could have a greater dispersion of political and economic power, a revitalized democratic process, and a new social contract for "humanistic capitalism." Multinational corporations have an important role to play in the transition, since they have a vested interest in the future well-being of the economy, have enormous economic power, have <u>entree</u> into national political institutions, and have the technical and financial resources to help in the process of learning and planning.

Small Is Beautiful: If we really followed the principle of subsidiary function--that a higher level should never do what a lower level can do and that the burden of proof always lies on those who want to deprive a lower level of its function--then the opposition between centralizing and dispersing decision-making power would be far behind us. Society would shift dramatically toward a dispersal of political and economic power to lower levels and smaller-scale institutions. The federal government, while decreasing in size and scope, would gain in authority and real effectiveness.

Minimum Feasible: Centralization of political and economic power is directly related to increasing use of energy. Beyond a certain level, power corrupts: those who have access to high energy levels will use it to maintain advantage and control. Capitalist firms with access to high energy will increase rapidly in scale, becoming national and international, and will no longer be controlled by a weak or decentralized political process. Government must become large and centralized if it is to attempt to regulate high-energy economic organizations, or, as in communist countries, to take them over. True participatory democracy is possible only in a low-energy society. Minimum feasible energy use is the only strategy by which a decentralized political process can keep limits on the power of even the most motorized capitalist or bureaucrat. Although people have begun to accept ecological limits on maximum percapita energy use, they do not yet think about the need for much lower energy limits as the necessary foundation for any truly democratic social order. Yet they are already experiencing, in their own lives, the fact that society has passed a threshold beyond which further energy inputs only act to increase feelings of individual impotence.

CIVIL LIBERTIES

Superindustrial: Energy and GNP growth cannot be stopped without a massive abridgment of civil liberties; continued economic health is the best guarantee of freedom. Innovative and manipulative social engineering will be increasingly applied to social, political, cultural, and economic areas by elites and specialists. We must be alert for unlikely but possible civil liberties problems involving computerized records, advanced surveillance techniques, nuclear technology safeguards, and so forth.

Plenitude: Danger to civil liberties in the transition period can be mitigated by widespread understanding of the need for a more frugal society and rapid value change so that a materially frugal, human-growth oriented society is perceived as a highly desirable goal.

Small Is Beautiful: Large-scale nuclear-power production poses grave threats to civil liberties because of the necessity for protection against the high risks of sabotage and plutonium theft. Background investigations, psychological testing, on-site personal searches, and other forms of security checks would be necessary for people who work at reactors, nuclear fuel processing plants, and other places where plutonium is stored and handled. Infiltration, mail covers, wiretapping, bugging, and other forms of covert surveillance would be necessary to keep track of terrorist groups, organized criminals, political dissidents, nuclear critics, and other groups that could be reasonably suspected of planning plutonium diversion or sabotage. When a situation of nuclear blackmail actually occurs, serious invasions of civil liberties would occur and would be accepted as necessary by reasonable people. A widely publicized nuclear threat or an actual incident of destruction would create public hysteria; history shows that constitutional rights do not fare well during such periods. In civil liberties, as in every other way, nuclear power is the antithesis of "small is beautiful."

Minimum Feasible: We are so conditioned that we do not realize that we already live in a totally programmed society. We have long since passed the level of energy use and GNP at which the cost of social control rises faster than the total output and becomes the major institutional activity within the economy. Once a critical quantum of energy is surpassed, conditioning for the abstract goals of bureaucracy becomes a stronger force than even the best legal guarantees of personal initiative. "Therapy" administered by educators, psychiatrists, and social workers will converge with the designs of planners, managers, and salesmen and will complement the operations of security agencies, the military, and the police. Major deviations from cultural programming will be severely punished, up to and including assassination.

VULNERABILITY OR STABILITY

Superindustrial: Current energy problems are of a transient socioeconomic rather than a physical or systemic nature, and their resolution will require only one or two decades at most, and possibly only a few years. If we are reasonably prudent, we will not have to contend with serious shortages in the medium run, and prospects for the long run are extremely encouraging. It is probably nonsense to believe that the poor will be strong enough to seize much of the wealth of the rich by force. But we must be on the alert for farfetched and unlikely but potentially dangerous events, such as ozone-layer destruction, a greenhouse effect, problems with nuclear wastes, large-scale ecological changes, million-ton oil spills, and growing guilt and alienation in the rich nations.

Plenitude: Current energy problems are one aspect of a systemic crisis in industrial civilizations which will come to a head during the

coming generation. Its resolution will eventually require an evolutionary transformation of ideas, values, and institutions toward a more
frugal, human-growth-oriented society. Continuation of current trends
will lead to radical instability. Massive use of nuclear power would
require a "nuclear priesthood" to maintain the safety of equipment and
wastes in a society whose stability could be assured for thousands of
years. Centralized nuclear power generation is also highly vulnerable
to sabotage. Nuclear fission, therefore, cannot ultimately be tolerated; its growth should be restricted, and present plants should redouble
engineering precautions and be phased out over time. Solar technology
can provide as high a level of energy as needed, with much less vulnerability.

Small Is Beautiful: The present industrial system is inherently
unstable because it consumes the very basis on which it has been erected:
nonrenewable energy sources, the tolerance margins of nature, and the
"human substance" itself. Social stability is especially neglected. To
motivate mankind for the single-minded pursuit of production and wealth,
modern society systematically cultivates the human vices of greed and
envy. The traditional folk wisdom and the highest religious teachings
of every past civilization warn that the consequence of cultivating greed
and envy is nothing less than a collapse of intelligence. Industrial
society is becoming increasingly vulnerable as it hypertrophies into
evolutionary dead ends of overspecialization, overcentralization and
highly interlocking systems susceptible to pyramiding catastrophes.

Minimum Feasible: Industrial society is nearing a crisis point.
Some of its elite are now vocally promulgating a limits-to-growth
ideology, which is highly undesirable because it pushes people to accept
limits to energy growth and industrial output without questioning the
basic structure of modern society, so that the growth-optimizing bureau-
crats may maintain their power. However, it is unlikely that many people
can be motivated by an abstract ideology to make major changes, and so
it is unlikely that a crash can be avoided.

PLURALIST OR HOMOGENEOUS SOCIETY

Superindustrial: World society is rapidly becoming more homogeneous:
westernized, modernized, industrialized; increasingly empirical, this-
worldly, secular, humanistic, pragmatic, manipulative, explicitly rational, quantitative, utilitarian, contractual, epicurean, hedonistic. There
has been a recent emergence, at least in the United States, of "mosaic"
cultures: incorporating exotic, deviant, communal, and experimental ways
of life. This so-called counterculture is a dangerous, premature, distorted introduction to upper-middle-class elites of some characteristics
of the coming post-industrial society. The influence of the counterculture is rapidly fading, and we are becoming, again, a nation of
"squares." This is good, because squares make great taxpayers, soldiers,
and citizens. They are realistic.

Plenitude: We need a high level of tolerance for diversity because
we are changing at a historically unprecedented pace and exploring ideas

for potential social transformation at every level, from individual consciousness to family and human settlement patterns to global institutions. A learning and planning society must be a pluralist society.
However, it is becoming clear that some key ideas, especially an ecological ethic and a self-realization ethic, need to be accepted widely.

Small Is Beautiful: People are right to be conservative, but the
label is often captured by ideas that go back only through a few political administrations. An unexpected alliance of younger social critics
who have thought of themselves as radical and older critics who have
thought of themselves as true conservatives is converging on a vision of
society based on the most ancient values of human scale: simplicity,
nonviolence, hard work, and restraint; space, sun, and trees, and beauty;
human dignity and forthright means; and basic truths of human experience
implicit in the teachings of the major world religions. Diversity is
of value as long as it exists within this basic framework of agreement.

Minimum Feasible: A low-energy policy allows for a wide choice of
lifestyles and cultures--as is evident in the variety of human history.
If, on the other hand, a society chooses high energy consumption, its
social relations must be dictated by technocracy and will be equally
distasteful whether labeled capitalist or socialist.

EQUITY

Superindustrial: Both the rich and the poor will get richer, and absolute poverty will be abolished during the twenty-first century, but some
will remain much richer than others. Americans must avoid feeling guilty
about the disproportionate consumption of global resources (they are
approximately 5 percent of the world's population using approximately
40 percent of global resources) because the high concentration of wealth
and consumption in the rich nations offers the only realistic hope that
the poor have for climbing out of poverty rapidly. Poorer countries can
draw on the rich, industrialized world for markets, capital, technology,
useful examples, experts, tourist wealth, and foreign aid, and for its
import of unskilled labor (which gives money and training to the
unskilled) and its export of industry, especially through the multinational corporation.

Plenitude: The expectations and demands of the developing nations
are rising rapidly under the impact of global communications, but the
gap probably cannot be closed by making poorer countries as productive,
consuming, energy-intensive, and polluting as the rich nations. If the
hopes of the world's poor continue to be frustrated while the rich become
steadily more extravagant, prospects for world peace will dim and terrorism (including nuclear terrorism), clashes over resources, and wars
of redistribution will become more likely. Above all, we need to change
direction in the United States toward a better example of what it means
to be a developed society: a materially frugal, humane society.
Required is a new concept of international economics that will embody the
idea that, just as individual nations establish mechanisms for redistribution of wealth and power, so must international society. Something

like Rawls' (1971) <u>A Theory of Justice</u>, whose central doctrine is to mitigate the effects of poverty, may become a key bargaining principle for both the rich and the poor, since it justifies inequality within limits while demanding improvement for the poorest. We need to find more effective, multilateral ways to help nations that want rapid industrialization, but we also need to be open to aiding nations--China, Burma, Vietnam, and others--that choose not to develop according to the western industrial model.

Small Is Beautiful: The greatest equity issue is intergenerational: we are exhausting fossil fuels, ruining soil fertility, unbalancing ecosystems, and distorting human values and institutions in the greatest energy-spending spree of all time, at the expense of future generations. Countries that begin their development processes later than others will be enormously disadvantaged by the earlier squandering of fossil fuels and the higher general level of prices. Global equity will not be served by aiding industrialization based on so-called advanced technology alone. Western-style industrialization in the poorer countries causes the formation of powerful elites living in small, ultramodern islands within a sea of poverty; destruction of the economic and social structure of the hinterland; mass migration into unmanageable urban slums; massive unemployment; destruction of the best features of traditional culture; debt; high dependence on, and control by, rich nations and multinational corporations; and many other problems. These problems can be avoided if the industrial nations aid the nonindustrial ones in developing an intermediate technology fitting between traditional immobility and materialistic modernization. Such a technology should seriously address the problem of general poverty and fully utilize the enthusiasm, intelligence, and labor power of everyone. It should be cheap, labor intensive, simple in its demand for skills, and appropriate for a diverse new form of agroindustrial society. It should promote advances in education, organization, and discipline so that more demanding technologies can be incorporated into general use over time.

Minimum Feasible: True equity requires the least feasible energy use by the most powerful members of society.

PROFESSIONALISM

Superindustrial: The use of professional elites for highest-quality performance of tasks is crucial. Professions are considered an important sector of economic growth, and an increase in student enrollments in business, law, medical, and other professional schools is encouraged. There is an emphasis on high-level certification, which is accomplished by internal "guild" criteria. Specialization continues because of an information explosion and rapidly increasing social complexity, and there is more emphasis on technical skills, on know-how. Professionals work in high-technology, "great project" professional work: SST development, organ transplants, megastructure architecture, nuclear engineering. Professionals concentrate in large institutions and urban areas.

Plenitude, Small Is Beautiful, Minimum Feasible (in order of increasing emphasis): Professionalism undergoes major modifications: There is a demystification of professional jargon; self-help and mutual care by nonprofessional laypeople becomes a core concept. An emphasis on preventive and holistic medicine decreases the need for doctors; a guaranteed annual income reduces the growth of professions that live off the ills of society. There is a broadening of professional education as an awareness of problems caused by complex bureaucracies and special-ized incompetence grows; there is, as well, more emphasis on holistic perspectives, values, knowing what to do. The emphasis on new profes-sional and paraprofessional roles, such as those of physicians' assistants and workers in self-help cooperatives, will require less formal training. Professional work will be judged increasingly by non-professional criteria: client satisfaction, social choices, and expectations defined in the political process and new and major shifts in societal values arising from outside the professions. There will be increasing emphasis on appropriate-technology, everyday-life-project professional work: preventive-medicine guidebooks, energy-efficient appliances, resource- and energy-conserving community-scale architecture. Community and family will support persons who can't "go it alone." Pro-fessionals will locate themselves according to need--they will be decentralized, with a concomitant revitalization of community, small towns, and smaller institutions.

REFERENCES

Armstrong, J. E., and W. W. Harman. 1975. Plausibility of a Restricted Energy Growth Scenario. Menlo Park, Calif.: Stanford Research Institute (CSSP 3705-8).

Callenbach, E. 1975. Ecotopia. Berkeley, Calif.: Banyan Tree Books.

Goodman, P., and P. Goodman. 1960. Communitas. Means of Livelihood and Ways of Life. New York: Vintage Books.

Harman, W. W. 1976. An Incomplete Guide to the Future. Stanford, Calif.: Stanford Alumni Association.

Illich, I. 1973. Tools for Conviviality. New York: Harper and Row.

Illich, I. 1974. Energy and Equity. New York: Harper and Row.

Kahn, H., and B. Bruce-Briggs. 1972. Things to Come: Thinking About the '70s and '80s. New York: Macmillan.

Kahn, J., W. Brown, and L. Martel. 1976. The Next 200 Years. New York: William Morrow.

Raskin, M., ed. 1973. Encyclopedia of Social Reconstruction. Institute for Policy Studies, Washington, D.C.

Rawls, J. 1971. A Theory of Justice. Cambridge, Mass.: Belknap Press.

Schumacher, E. F. 1973. Small Is Beautiful. New York: Harper and Row.

Turnbull, C. 1961. The Forest People. London: Chatto and Windbus.

3   TO SUPPLY ENERGY: BREEDER REACTORS

This chapter and the following one ring another set of changes on the
central theme of this book: that decisions about energy cannot rest
solely on economic considerations but must rather be made in the context
of cultural values. In these chapters we focus on issues of energy
supply.

Our speculations about the future emphasize matters of technology,
of institutional factors, and of the kind of society in which we might
want to live. In setting this emphasis, we do not mean to ignore cost
considerations. We recognize, though, that cost-estimation techniques
are so deficient in many situations that it is simply not meaningful to
suggest that decisions among many technologies can be realistically
based on cost. Cost estimates for new technologies are inevitably optimistic, for new technologies in prototype are always expensive, and
imaginative engineers can always see routes to dramatic cost reduction.
Sometimes these occur, as happened with transistors. But sometimes costs
do not drop. The French and British experience with the SST illustrates
this, as does experience in all nations with costs of nuclear systems.

Present estimates of the costs of delivering electricity from coal
and nuclear systems are extraordinarily close. For our part, no cost
numbers are credible--at least not within a range that would let us
decide clearly and unambiguously between solar and nuclear systems. If
societal costs could be included, it is possible that they might shift
the balance.

In any case, we believe that the decisions facing our society
as we move from the fossil-fuel era to the era of renewable resources
transcend cost considerations. Far more important are the implications of our choice of an energy system for the availability of
energy, social stability, individual freedom, and relations of the

United States with developing nations.[a] It is to these issues rather than to cost which we urge the reader to address his or her attention.

ENERGY SOURCES: THE ALTERNATIVES

We must look to alternative sources of energy because we assume that global reserves of oil and natural gas are finite and that the end of the oil and gas era is close at hand. Precisely when oil and gas production will reach their peak on a global basis depends on exploration rates, the total global resource base, and the rate of growth in world demand (Figs. 1 and 2). Such analyses have been carried out by various groups, of which the early work of Hubbert (1974) and the recent analysis by the Workshop on Alternative Energy Strategies (1976) provide a good overview and examination of the potential consequences for the world.

We assume that the transition from increasing to decreasing our reliance on oil and natural gas will take place in this century or early in the next. If the United States decides to lower its demand for energy, as in either the 72-quad or the 53-quad scenario described in this report, it will extend the time in which we must begin the transition to renewable energy forms. This timing is of course affected by actions throughout the world, but if the United States were to lead the way by basing its economic system on energy resources that will be available over the long term, other nations might choose similarly, just as other nations have followed the United States's lead in developing nuclear power. The important symbolic nature of the United States's choice is not amenable to technical analysis.

Major investments will be required by our society so that we can avoid substantial dislocations as we move to other energy forms. Coal and nonbreeder nuclear power are the prime candidates usually considered for bridging the gap. Unfortunately, both entail major environmental and capital difficulties. In spite of this, these technologies play significant roles in the views of many of the planners who are now advising our political leadership.

In the longer term there are few choices open. Coal could provide us with perhaps a century of respite but new technologies for reducing coal's environmental impacts will be needed if coal is to be our main energy source. Reliance on coal also presupposes that we find some way to abate coal's potential for modifying global climatic conditions by its emissions of carbon dioxide.

Limitations on the supply of uranium place corresponding limits on its application for nonbreeder nuclear systems. Fusion-energy systems currently present formidable technological difficulties that may forever prevent their operating. Should such systems become a reality, their

---

[a] For a guide to citizen participation in decision making see Nader and Abbotts (1977). For a discussion of science and the determination of safety, see Lowrance (1976). For a discussion of world energy strategies, see Lovins (1976b).

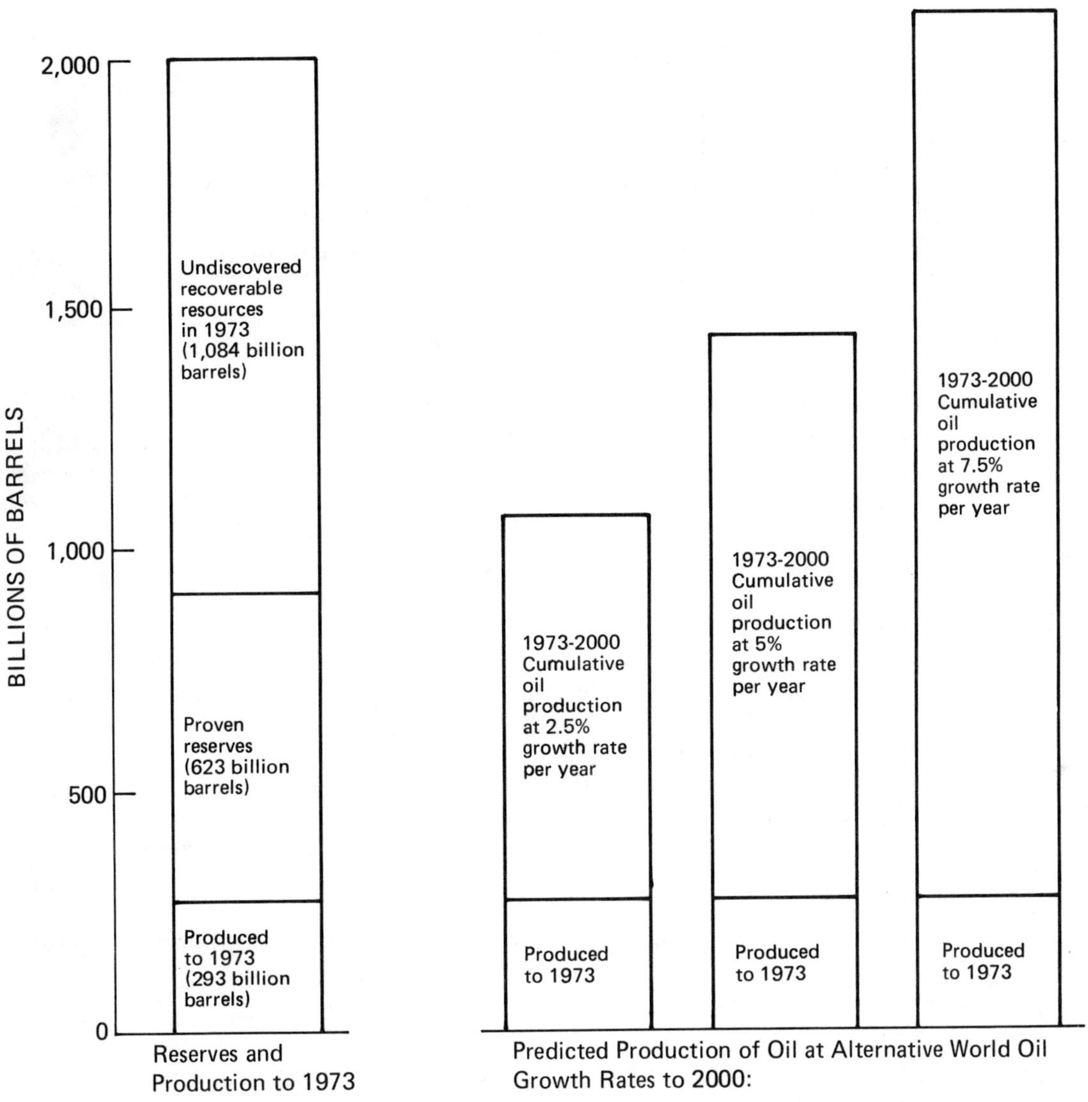

Figure 1 Cumulative world oil production to 2000 (Moody and Geiger)

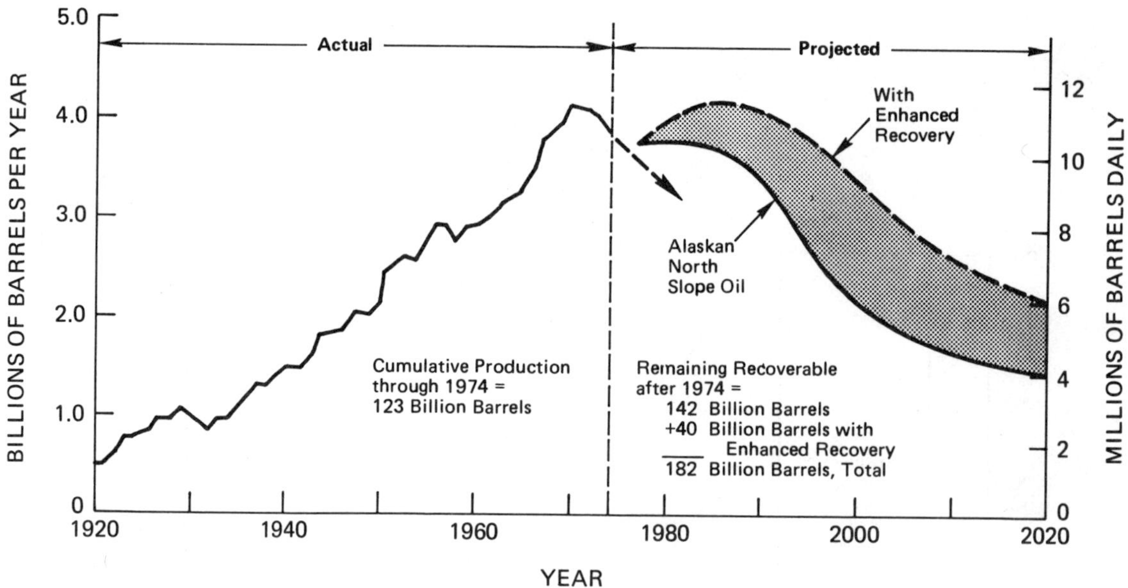

Figure 2 Projected production of domestic oil, including crude oil
and natural-gas liquids (U.S. Energy Research and Development,
1975)

environmental and social problems may well prove comparable with those
of conventional nuclear-reactor systems. We have excluded discussion
of both kinds of system.

Breeder reactors are, according to many, the most promising long-
term choice.

Other long-term approaches are geothermal and solar energy. Of
these, solar technologies appear closer to reality as sources of large
amounts of energy.

From among these numerous possibilities, we have chosen to examine
solar-energy systems and breeder-reactor systems. We emphasize these
energy-supply mixes because they illustrate fundamentally different
directions in which our society might move. Both are for practical purposes unlimited in the amounts of energy that they can supply. Both
appear capable of supplying energy over limitless periods of time. Both
technologically and institutionally, however, they are at opposite
extremes.

In this chapter, we examine some of the social effects likely to
follow a major commitment to nuclear breeder reactors. Chapter 4 focuses
on ways in which alternative value systems might lead to an energy-supply
system that is based on renewable resources and is capable, if necessary,
of meeting high-energy requirements but uses predominantly solar-energy
technologies.

THE NUCLEAR-BREEDER PATH

Capital Intensity

Breeder reactors have useful lives of about 30 years. Each spent hulk
must be maintained and guarded. It appears likely that each new reactor requires an entirely new site, but there is no current research to
lead to an informed conclusion. These costs of installation, of continuing maintenance, of security and custodial care, and of fuel and
waste processing make the breeder reactor even more capital intensive
than other forms of nuclear-power production, which are extremely capital intensive.

In terms of national policy, perhaps the most important consequence
of installing breeder reactors to provide more than a small fraction of
our energy is that a commitment to a breeder-reactor system is an unbreak-
able commitment. Once vast amounts of capital have been invested in
breeder power plants, fuel-reprocessing plants, fuel-enrichment plants,
and so on, a retreat from this energy system while the breeder fuel lasts
will be difficult economically, no matter what the considerations of
health, safety, environment, and social effects turn out to be. This
point cannot be stressed enough: investing in a national breeder-reactor
system is a major investment, and changing our minds will be exceedingly
difficult, if not impossible.

The vast sums of capital necessary to build, keep building, maintain,
care for, and guard such systems must be raised somehow. The inflation-
ary effects of huge simultaneous bond issues, federally appropriated
moneys, private loans, projected rising fuel costs, and proliferating
custodial and police costs will give a major and perhaps unwelcome jolt
to the economy.

Capital-intensive systems are usually lightly manned. Therefore
fewer people will probably be directly employed in energy-producing
areas with nuclear power than with technologies, such as coal, that are
more labor intensive. However, many more people will be employed in
the security forces necessary to guard breeder-reactor systems. This
pattern of few working and many policing can be expected to produce
growing resentment in an economy in which there is serious unemployment
in industries that consume large amounts of energy.

A final effect of the need for massive capitalization is that many
social-service programs may be eliminated or severely curtailed. If
too much of the available money in the economy is preempted to construct
nuclear power plants and related facilities, cutbacks of considerable
magnitude can be expected in Social Security, Medicare, veterans' benefits, food programs, FHA loans and insurance, and so on. People who
depend on these social buffers for survival will justifiably feel that
they are being deprived so that others who are already wealthy may
profit.

Centralization: The Bureaucracy

Nuclear power is heavily regulated and controlled by the federal government. The huge amounts of federal capital necessary for the establishment of a large-scale nuclear-power system will increase federal involvement even more. Meeting the safety requirements of a nuclear system in addition will generate unprecedented federal regulations and control. That a federal regulatory agency will dominate a national breeder-reactor system is taken for granted by all planners. The size of such an agency would have to be immense.

It is well known that, up to a certain point, the bigger a system is, the more economically it can produce a given unit of its product, be that product electricity or administrative supervision. Beyond a certain limit, for physical facilities as well as for human organizations, an increase in size actually makes a unit of the same product more expensive.

The point of diminishing returns may not yet have been reached for reactors. Bigger reactors may yet produce electricity more cheaply. However, it is quite clear that the point of diminishing returns for bureaucratic structures has been passed. The federal government contains many agencies that spend so much time and money on internal communication, internal accounting, and internal administration that they find it increasingly expensive to attend to the external duties that are their reasons for existence.

The nuclear regulatory agency that a national commitment to breeder-reactor power would require would unquestionably be large and unwieldly. It would also be expensive; this expense is a cost not often considered in discussions of nuclear power. Finally, the administrative mission of such an agency would be inherently contradictory. On the one hand, capital and safety considerations, as well as the need to reconcile regional differences about the assets and liabilities of nuclear power, would demand a single centralized agency. On the other hand, regional and local differences in power needs and costs, safety considerations, and other matters could only with great difficulty be handled by a single agency with a single set of policies. Attempts to manage such contradictions are likely to exacerbate internal communication problems, and, in time, to increase the agency's size.

Another matter of considerable concern to students of politics is the possibility of an "internal OPEC," consisting of a consortium of private nuclear-power companies and their allies in a hopelessly inefficient and/or co-opted regulatory agency. Given the long-established practice of recruiting the members of regulatory commissions from, and returning them to, top-level jobs in the industries they are designated to regulate, this concern is genuine. Such an alliance would be able to raise energy prices almost at will and perhaps even to deny energy to political or commercial opponents.

Faced by the present giant bureaucracy, many individuals already believe that they have practically no influence on energy prices or policy. A new and surpassingly large agency, particularly one with as

much authority to regulate as would be possessed by a national energy
commission, could lead citizens to believe the agency was in collusion
with the power companies. The very real complaint of citizens' lack
of local authority, or even influence, in decisions that affect their
lives would proceed through suspicions of citizens' being exploited, to
a final conviction that the people in charge of a national nuclear-power
establishment are personally corrupt. Public acceptance of such a large
governmental structure could no doubt be enforced, but it is highly ques-
tionable that acceptance would be more than a cynical acknowledgment
that there is nothing to be done about it.

Centralization:
Technological Vulnerability and Site Proliferation

A system of nuclear breeder reactors would probably be constructed by
clustering the units to take advantage of economies of scale and to
facilitate security. Breeder power would thus involve large plants
serving larger areas than those now accommodated by our national power
grid. To construct a nuclear system otherwise would aggravate the
already staggering construction costs. (See Lovins, 1976a, for deeper
consideration of these issues.)

Such centralization of power supply, or even the interlocking of
small supply units, increases the vulnerability of large areas to a
failure anywhere in the system, as the Northeastern blackouts demonstrated. The Northeastern blackout of 1965 was resolved within a matter
of hours; the blackout of 1977 was more prolonged. But the usual sort
of reactor accident requires closing the plant for an extended period,
perhaps permanently. Because of the large size of nuclear grids, even
more people would be affected than were concerned in the Northeast.
Such an accident could also occur during the winter. Technological vulnerability may seem too high a price to pay for breeder reactors when we
realize that a reactor accident might deprive us of electric power at
the very moment when several million people would need to be evacuated
from the area in which the accident had taken place.

The 30-year life of a breeder necessitates the continuing construction of new reactors and the care and guarding of the spent hulks. A
natural reluctance to build new reactors in as-yet-uncontaminated areas
might lead to new plants' being built at some minimum safe distance from
recently abandoned ones. A number of constantly enlarging "nuclear bad-
lands" would thus be created, expanding perhaps dangerously close to
the major population centers that the centralized generating facilities
are designed to serve.

Legal Effects of Safety Considerations

Much recent discussion has centered on the effect of nuclear safety considerations on the civil rights and civil liberties of individuals. The
dangers of theft from, or sabotage of, a plutonium facility are so great

that drastic invasions of individual freedom will be required, according to an extensive review by Ayres (1975), who sees the issue as stretching from incursions into the civil liberties of a few thousand reactor employees, who are subject to wiretap, covert surveillance, lie detector tests, and so on as a condition of holding their jobs, to the warrantless search, imprisonment, and perhaps brutal interrogation of virtually unlimited numbers of people living in the vicinity of a plutonium theft or of a threat of sabotage.

Ayres is somewhat conservative. He does not consider, for instance, the security measures that would be necessary along roads carrying trucks transporting plutonium. Nor does he give much attention to the likelihood of greatly expanded powers for private police forces employed by the privately owned reactor companies, who would enjoy a status for which the legal avenues of responsibility are rather unclear, given the joint federal and private character of their work.

One is chilled by the specter of a double line of armed men standing shoulder to shoulder along both sides of a highway for several hundred miles, protecting a truck carrying plutonium-bearing fuel rods. And yet, given the fact that plutonium need not be made into a bomb to accomplish mass destruction but can simply be dispersed into the atmosphere by a single high-explosive charge, such as a mortar shell, without the attacker's ever touching the object of his assault, such an imagined scene is not unrealistic.

Safety considerations, so vital in dealing with breeder-produced plutonium, would undoubtedly have the following consequences: (1) restrictive laws dealing with all aspects of behavior in the vicinity of facilities that produce, store, process, and transport plutonium; (2) a large increase in the number of police throughout the country, or alternatively, a vastly increased civilian role for the army; (3) police use of plutonium safety considerations to justify extraordinary investigative, arrest, and regulatory measures for suspected nonnuclear crimes and disapproved behavior; and (4) some increase in central, federal direction of local law enforcement, although not necessarily with an equal increase in federal accountability by local levels of those authorities.

Future Generations

Both the assets and the liabilities of a breeder-reactor system will fall more heavily on future generations than on anyone living today (Speth, Tamplin, and Cochran, 1974). Others have discussed in great detail the dangers to our children's health and to the natural environment that would follow a decision to build breeder reactors. But something deserves to be said about the social environment that children in a society relying on nuclear fuel will inherit. A society using a large-scale breeder system as its primary energy source will be more centralized, more regimented, and more elitist than the American society of today. Trends in this direction have been noticeable for a long time in American life and show no sign of abating. They may in fact be inevitable to some extent. Nevertheless, the degree to which these trends

will be accelerated by a plutonium economy seems to be nearly without
precedent. The difference in degree may be such that it will rapidly
result in a difference in kind. It is not impossible that America will
find her children growing up in a society so stratified and regimented
that it more nearly resembles fifteenth-century Peru or nineteenth-
century Prussia than the twentieth-century United States.

International Effects

A decision by the United States to eschew nuclear power would probably
not stimulate similar decisions by other nations; nor would it slow the
proliferation of nuclear bombs. However, a strong commitment by the
United States to rely on nuclear power could accelerate the accumula-
tion of, and experimentation with, fissionable material by other nations,
particularly those of the Third World. No advantage at all is to be
gained in maintaining one's country as a nuclear-free zone when unlimited amounts of fissionable material are being produced on the same
planet. Only when the total amount of fissionable material everywhere
is relatively limited can a country persuade itself that, at least for
the moment, it is safer to avoid the whole issue of nuclear fission.

Energy and Social Structure

Anthropologists have observed that those who control scarce but necessary resources control the society that depends on those resources.
Nonfood energy has been a necessity in our society since the industrial
revolution. The centralized and capital-intensive nature of breeder-
reactor technology implies that the relatively few people who will control energy production will in roughly equal measure come to dominate
the political scene. Current aspirations to grass-roots control will
be frustrated, and access to real political power will be limited to a
very few.

An analogy from recent United States history underscores the point.
From around the turn of the nineteenth century and until somewhat later,
railroads completely dominated large-scale transportation in this country. The owners of railroad companies also dominated political life to
an extraordinary degree. At the grass-roots level there was a distrust
and outright hatred of the railroad companies and their owners, which
brought our country closer perhaps than we have ever been to class war-
fare. Nevertheless, building railroads had to be done through capital-
intensive means and under highly centralized control. No alternative
measures could have succeeded, for the railroads were expensive for
their time.

The power of the railroads was in time diminished, not only by
federal regulation, but also by the rise of a viable alternative in
motor vehicles and public roads. Private trucks and cars broke the
monopoly of a small segment of the population on the scarce resource
of long-distance transportation. No one any longer hates the railroads
as Frank Norris (1901) did, nor does anyone hate the several dozen

medium-sized trucking companies that distribute a large share of our national freight.

The parallel with breeder reactors and other energy technologies is limited, however, for we shall not be able to build anything comparable with the system of public roads if our new railroads create the sorts of social problems that the old ones did. The capital that a breeder system will siphon away from other areas will reduce our monetary resources to such an extent that we shall not be able to afford alternatives. Aware of the system's terrible vulnerability, people might come to hate the breeders and their managers so much that they would be willing to suffer any cost to remove them.

Who Will Watch the Watchers?

The question of centralization--of hardware, of bureaucracy, of political and economic power--may ultimately be the most important energy policy issue. The commitment to a national breeder-reactor energy system would entail not only the exercise of greater and more centralized power by the government, but also the assumption of a much greater share of that power by the scientists, technicians, and administrators who would man the system. This prospect may be particularly attractive to the scientists who, in a country that has traditionally given its intellectuals influence and prestige but not power, suddenly find themselves confronted with the giddy possibility of attaining a sizable amount of real power. It would be only human for them to assume that the social consequences of choosing a breeder system would be as beneficial as, or at least would enhance, the technical consequences. They would, of course, reach such a conclusion convinced of the purity of their own motives and of the opportunities for improving the common good that would thus be offered to people of their talents and good will in positions of real power.

It would be foolish in the extreme to assume that nuclear scientists are power-hungry monsters. It would be equally foolish to assume that they are able to make a dispassionate assessment of a situation in which they stand to gain or lose a great deal. The sociopolitical consequences of a commitment to a breeder-reactor system are an area in which the advice of the experts must be accepted with more than one grain of salt (Holdren, 1976). An informed political judgment in this area can come only from the advice of the broadest possible cross section of the population, and that advice can be meaningful only if it is based on a full appreciation of the likely sociopolitical impacts of the breeder reactor.

BREEDER REACTORS AND SOLAR-ENERGY SYSTEMS: SOME CONTRASTS

Breeder reactors appear particularly well suited to the production of electricity. Under certain circumstances they could provide industrial process heat, but the large size of proposed breeder systems makes it unlikely that there will be more than a limited number of nonelectric applications.

Solar-energy systems are extremely well suited for providing process heat, particularly for industrial processes requiring low temperatures. The solar-energy systems that we consider are best suited to provide climate conditioning, low-temperature process heat, and hot water. Electrical energy produced from solar sources will, without major advances, remain considerably more expensive than energy produced by using other applications of solar energy.

According to the CONAES Solar Resource Group (National Research Council, 1979a) and the Demand and Conservation Panel (National Research Council, 1979b), solar systems for domestic and industrial heating could, before the end of the century, become economically competitive (within the context of the quadrupled-energy-price assumptions of the Demand and Conservation Panel). The cost of breeder-produced electricity is also expected to become competitive with those of other electricity sources, according to the estimates of the CONAES Supply and Delivery Panel (National Research Council, 1979c).

The two systems differ markedly in terms of the institutional problems associated with their implementation and operation. Solar systems make use of simple technology, widely distributed. The breeder technologies are exceedingly complex and contain many elements (e.g., the reactor itself, the fuel-supply chain, fuel transport and reprocessing, and radioactive-waste storage), all of which must operate in unison if the overall system is to operate safely. The solar technologies can be installed and maintained by workers of modest skill. The breeder systems will require highly trained workers and an institutional structure capable of operating flawlessly for generations.

It is possible to imagine a steady-state society operating on long-term energy forms in which electrical energy is produced by breeder reactors while virtually all other forms of energy derive from solar systems. However, the institutional and technical aspects of breeder and of solar-energy systems are so different that it is not at all clear whether the two types of system could coexist. Whether institutional mechanisms that would permit this could be developed is a matter of conjecture.

A variety of considerations could move the emphasis of the debate concerning the nation's energy system away from the economics of massive new technologies, such as coal gasification and nuclear power. A decision to move toward renewable resources could be viewed as the nation's rational response to the end of the era of oil and gas. Such a national commitment might be viewed as comparable with the decision made in the Middle Ages to build cathedrals, the decision made by the United States in the 1960's to put a man on the moon, or the decisions to defend the nation in the First and Second World Wars. The pressures that will be imposed on the nation as a result of the depletion of oil and gas have few historic analogs. But if a national commitment develops, it can lead to major investments of national resources to accomplish objectives viewed by the nation at large as important national goals.

SUMMARY

As we said earlier, those who control scarce but necessary resources control the society that depends on those resources. In the case of the breeder, control extends well into the future, and along with other vulnerable technologies may generate hazardous conditions that are not easily reversible. To summarize:

1. Once set in motion, a national breeder-reactor system would be difficult to dismantle because of the great amount of capital invested in building and maintaining it.

2. Intergenerational injustices of an essentially irreversible decision should be a primary concern.

3. Large-scale bureaucratic centralization and proliferation would be an inevitable product of a national breeder system.

4. A centralization of political power, attendant on the centralized capitalization and operation of facilities, custodial care, and guarding of spent hulks and fuel and waste systems may well result in massive political disaffection at the grass-roots level.

5. Technological centralization would also result, thereby increasing vulnerability to accident and sabotage.

6. Safety considerations would compel drastic reductions in civil rights, with a general increase in numbers and power of police. The total number of reactors will not affect this general pattern.

7. Breeder sites may be unavailable for renewal, and this feature could involve the need to guard thousands of acres of dead land.

8. The nature of this technology can have marked effects on government organization and civil rights. Political disaffection may combine with extreme centralization and elitism to produce a society unlike the America of today and repugnant to the political ideals of this country to date.

9. There is a possibility of an "internal OPEC" of nuclear energy producers that would wield unprecedented power.

10. There is an even stronger likelihood that people will believe that such an internal OPEC exists, even if it does not.

11. The capital for a breeder-reactor system may have to come from the social-service sector of the economy, which, many believe, is already undersupported.

12. More public debate is needed.

REFERENCES

Ayres, R. 1975. Policing Plutonium: The Civil Liberties Fallout. Harvard Civil Rights-Civil Liberties Law Review 10(2):369-443.

Holdren, J. 1976. The Nuclear Controversy and the Limitation of Decision Making by Experts. Bulletin of Atomic Scientists 32(3):20-22.

Hubbert, M. 1974. U.S. Energy Resources: A Review as of 1972, Pt. 1. In A National Fuels and Energy Policy Study. U.S. Congress, Senate, Committee on Interior and Insular Affairs. Serial No. 93-40 (92-75). Washington, D.C.: U.S. Government Printing Office.

Lovins, A. 1976a. Scale, Centralization and Electrification in Energy Systems. In Future Strategies for Energy Development: A Question of Scale. Oak Ridge, Tenn.: Oak Ridge Associated Universities.

Lovins, A. 1976b. World Energy Strategies. Cambridge, Mass.: Ballinger.

Lowrance, W. W. 1976. Of Acceptable Risk. Los Altos, Calif.: William Kaufman.

Moody, J. D., and R. E. Geiger. 1975. Petroleum Resources: How Much Oil and Where. Technology Review 77(5)(March/April):38-45.

Nader, R., and J. Abbotts. 1977. The Menace of Atomic Energy. New York: W. W. Norton.

National Research Council. 1979a. Domestic Potential of Solar and Other Renewable Energy Sources. Solar Resource Group, Supply and Delivery Panel, Committee on Nuclear and Alternative Energy Systems. Supporting Paper 6. Washington, D.C.: National Academy of Sciences.

National Research Council. 1979b. Alternative Energy Demand Futures to 2010. Demand and Conservation Panel, Committee on Nuclear and Alternative Energy Systems. Washington, D.C.: National Academy of Sciences.

National Research Council. 1979c. U.S. Energy Supply Prospects to 2010. Supply and Delivery Panel, Committee on Nuclear and Alternative Energy Systems. Washington, D.C.: National Academy of Sciences.

Norris, F. 1901. The Octopus: Story of California. Garden City, N.Y.: Sun Dial Press.

Speth, J. G., A. R. Tamplin, and T. B. Cochran. 1974. Plutonium Recycle, the Fateful Step. Bulletin of Atomic Scientists 30(9):15-22.

U.S. Energy Research and Development Administration. 1975. A National Plan for Energy Research, Development, and Demonstration: Creating Energy Choices for the Future. Washington, D.C.: U.S. Government Printing Office (ERDA-48).

Workshop on Alternative Energy Strategies. 1976. Energy Demand Studies: Major Consuming Countries. Cambridge, Mass.: MIT Press.

4 TO SUPPLY ENERGY: THE SUN

Chapter 3's discussion of the breeder reactor drew upon the themes of
safety, liberty, and institutional structure because the decisions about
the nuclear breeder will no longer be determined solely on the scientific engineering and economic grounds that have in the past been central.
This chapter's discussion of solar technologies includes consideration
of feasibility issues, costs, organizational constraints, and societal
impacts of solar energy because these are the variables that are discussed increasingly in any debate on what is to happen after fossil fuels
can no longer serve as our main energy sources.

Until recently, solar energy and renewable technologies did not
receive serious attention. In spite of the obvious fact that the sun
shines every day, considerations of solar energy have been eclipsed by
the focus on more conventional, high technologies such as nuclear fission. The State of Connecticut, though, receives approximately as much
energy from the sun each year as the entire nation used from all nonfood
forms of energy during 1972. To phrase it differently, and more force-
fully, one barrel of oil contains as much chemical energy as the sun
supplies to each square meter of land in the United States each year.
There is no question that solar energy is abundant now and that it will
be available to human beings for as long as we might need it.

In spite of this, no one can say with assurance what energy impact
solar technology would have on the U.S. economy. The writers of this
report believe that if a national decision were made to encourage a
rapid transition to renewable resources, solar energy could be far more
significant than most energy forecasts indicate. As we view the matter,
most of the forecasts to date were made by groups with a strong technology orientation; they have emphasized high-technology uses for solar
energy, mainly for generating electricity, which we believe to be the
least economic use of solar energy at present.

On the contrary, we emphasize other sorts of uses for solar energy and compare our view with those of other forecasters.[a] Unfortunately, such forecasters rarely speak about the social impact of solar-energy technology or its consequent effect on social organization. Although the cost of energy development involves more than Btu's and dollars per Btu, we have developed our discussion within conventional boundaries—cost and use—in order to set the stage for reader participation in the scenario chapters that follow. The assumption that undergirds the scenario chapters, however, is that society is interconnected and evolves systemically. A shift in the direction of husbanding energy resources through energy conservation, an alteration in consumption habits, the development of renewable energy sources such as solar and geothermal—all these need to be seen in a systemic context. Energy systems impinge upon economic growth, the prospects of war and peace, and the degree of tension between countries.[b] But in this chapter on solar power, we turn to some rather straightforward questions: To what uses can solar energy be put? How soon can solar technology be available? How much would solar systems cost? Are there geographic variations? What are the implications of decentralization and scale? What are the broader constraints and possible incentives?

TO WHAT USES CAN SOLAR ENERGY BE PUT?

The most effective uses for solar energy are in space and water heating and in providing heat for industrial processes. Solar air conditioning is less well developed but could become commercially competitive over the next decade or so. Solar generation of electricity is a far less effective use; although technically feasible, it is expected to be much too costly to compete in the market for some years.

Our estimates of the extent to which solar energy could replace nonrenewable sources are extrapolations from the CONAES Demand and Conservation Panel's (1976) scenario B (which depends on a quadrupling of energy

---

[a]A substantial portion of this section is from material developed by W. Harman of Stanford Research Institute as a part of a report to the Energy Research and Development Administration assessing the impacts of the ERDA Solar Energy Program (Stanford Research Institute, 1976). We thank Mr. Harman for his kind permission to use this material. Our solar energy discussion reproduces cost estimates from the Solar Resource Group (1976) of CONAES and from the Demand and Conservation Panel (1976).

[b]The timing of the peak in oil and gas production on a global basis depends on exploration rates, total global resource base, and the rate of growth and demand not only in the United States but throughout the world. Such analyses have been carried out by various groups, of which the early work of Hubbert (1974) and the recent analysis by the Workshop on Alternative Energy Strategies (1976) provides a good overview and analysis of the potential consequences for the world. An energy future for the United States that is constrained to minimum demand growth for energy extends the amount of time available before a transition to renewable energy forms.

prices between 1975 and 2010). Tables 5 and 6, later in this section, are summaries of the two differing estimates. Like the CONAES Panel, we assume that the GNP will grow at an average rate of 2 percent per year through 2010.

Buildings and industry are the two sectors of the economy in which solar energy can have an impact.

Buildings Sector

In 1975 there were 70 million residential housing units in the United States; we assume that in 2010 there will be 133 million units, an increase of 63 million. Because of demolition, new housing starts between 1975 and 2010 will in fact be greater than this: 93 million units. Thus 70 percent of the units that will exist in 2010 do not now exist, and only about 57 percent of the units standing in 1975 will exist in 2010.

The thermal integrity of the new units is improved over that of existing units. By 2010 new residential units will use only about 75 percent as much heat as present units; commercial, educational, and government buildings will use 40 to 60 percent as much, depending on building type.

Starting in 1980, solar systems will begin to be installed, and by 2010 solar systems will be installed in 75 percent of new buildings. After 1980, new buildings will comprise 65 percent of the total building stock. On the basis of linear growth in GNP, we assume that solar systems will be installed in half of this 65 percent, or 32 percent of all buildings. We further assume that solar energy can meet 75 percent of the total demand for space and water heating and air conditioning in these buildings.

Scenario B (Demand and Conservation Panel, 1976), on the other hand, assumes that solar space and hot water heat, as well as solar air conditioning, will not come into wide use as quickly. By 2010, 10 percent of new air conditioners, 25 percent of new space heaters, and 50 percent of new water heaters will be solar. Scenario B projects for the buildings sector that total energy use from all sources in these categories will be 25.1 quads by 2010. Only 3 percent of that total, or 0.9 quad, is considered to be the maximum contribution by solar energy.

In our view, however, based on the above-stated assumptions, solar energy can meet 75 percent of the total 25.1 quad demand in 32 percent of the new buildings and can thus displace 6.0 quads of conventional energy sources.

Table 1 summarizes scenario B's analysis of energy uses in the buildings sector.

Table 1 Energy use, in quads[a], in buildings sector, according to
Demand and Conservation Panel scenario B

Use	Year	
	1975	2010
Space heating	12.6	16.6
Water heating	2.4	4.4
Air conditioning	1.8	4.1
Other (mostly electric)	7.9	13.1
Total	24.7	38.2
Residential	16.5	22.2
Nonresidential	8.2	16.0
Total	24.7	38.2
Primary energy per unit of housing stock[b]	234 million Btu	167 million Btu
Primary energy per square foot of floor space[c]	0.3 " "	0.2 " "

[a]Unless otherwise specified

[b]Assumes increase from 70.4 million to 133 million units of housing
stock.

[c]Commercial, educational and government buildings. Assumes increase
from 27 billion to 82 billion square feet of floor space.

Source: Adapted from Demand and Conservation Panel (1976)

Industrial Sector

Energy used in industrial processes accounted for about one-fourth of
primary energy consumed in the United States in 1975. Experts consider
that the industrial sector can use solar energy for most processes that
use heat at low temperatures. Three analyses have been made of the extent
to which solar energy can replace oil to provide heat at these low temperatures.

Battelle Columbus Laboratories and InterTechnology Corporation conducted process-heat analyses for the United States (Table 2) similar to that carried out for Canada by Lovins (1976).

Table 2 Process energy use in United States industry in 1975

Temperature range		Batelle/Columbus Laboratories (Process analysis)		InterTechnology Corporation (Statistical analysis)[a]	
		quads per year	percent	quads per year	percent
< 100°C (212°F):	Total	0.17	2	0.26	3
Hot water		0.07		0.12	
Direct heat		0.1		0.14	
100-177°C:	Total	1.34	17	3.25	32
Steam		1.2		2.6	
Direct heat		0.14		0.65	
> 177°C (350°F):	Total	6.35	81	6.53	65
Steam		0.5		0.56	
Direct heat		5.85		5.97	
Total		7.86	99[b]	10.04	100

[a]These figures include about 80% of all process heat; about 20% is in unexamined small industries with unknown temperature distribution.

[b]Total does not add due to rounding.

Source: Adapted from Lovins (1976)

Table 2 shows that in 1975 between 17 and 32 percent of all process-heat energy identified was used at temperatures below 350°F. Thus about 6 quads of energy now used in industry at low temperatures might be produced by using solar technologies.

The CONAES Solar Resource Group (1976) carried out an analogous investigation (Table 3) and concluded that 9.5 quads of process heat used in 1975 could be supplied by solar energy. By 2010, they estimated, solar energy could be used for 12 quads of process heat. However, they estimated a high 76 quads for total industrial-sector use.

Table 3 Projected U.S. total and process energy use, in quads per year

| Use | Year | | | | |
---	1975	1985	1990	2000	2010
Total energy use	75	98	112	146	190
Total industrial use	30	39	45	58	76
Total process heat	19	25	28	36	48
Steam/hot water/hot air for solar-favorable industries	9.5	12.5	14	18	24
Steam/hot water/hot air for solar-favorable industries in "sunshine" areas	4.7	6.2	7	9	12

[a]A growth rate in all categories of 2.7 percent per year over 35 years is assumed.

Source: Adapted from National Research Council (1979)

    The CONAES Demand and Conservation Panel (1976) also examined process heat in the six leading industries (Table 4). Of the total 19 quads used in these industries in 1975, 9.8 quads are for low-temperature steam and hot water, of which 8.1 quads are candidates for replacement by solar energy. In other words, solar energy could have replaced 12.5 percent of U.S. industrial energy usage in 1975.
    Since the industrial sector is expected to grow more rapidly than other sectors, a corresponding impact of 8 quads in 2010 appears to be a conservative estimate.
    We conclude that, with the support of a vigorous governmental policy, solar energy could replace 8 quads of oil in producing industrial process heat in 2010.

Biomass

The conversion of biomass to forms useful for meeting United States energy needs is extremely promising but singularly difficult to evaluate. Among the estimates are these from the CONAES Solar Resource Group: municipal wastes (1.7 quads), agricultural residues (3.5 quads), terrestrial energy

Table 4 1975 process heat use among six leading industrial users

Type of industry	Total use (quads)	Percentage in steam/ hot water	Energy in steam/hot water (quads)
Primary metals	4.2	21	0.9
Chemicals	4.0	60	2.4[a]
Petroleum	1.9	35	0.7
Stone, clay and glass	1.7	8	0.14
Paper and pulp	1.7	85	1.4[a]
Food processing	1.3	~90	1.2[a]
All others	4.2	~73	3.1[a]
Total	19.0		9.8

[a]Best solar candidates; total 8.1 quads

Source: Data from Dow Chemical (1975); Unger (1975)

crops (3.4 quads), and marine energy crops (1.1 quads). Conversion techniques include anaerobic digestion, pyrolysis, hydrolysis and fermentation, and direct combustion. Methane, methanol, and other gaseous or liquid fuels can be produced by all these processes except combustion.

The combined impact of biomass conversion for 2010, according to the estimates listed, is 9.7 quads. Because of the uncertain state of many of the technologies, we estimate a conservative 3 quads from all biomass sources.

Solar Electricity

Electricity production using solar technologies is the most uncertain of all. Electricity generated by solar thermal plants is currently estimated by some to cost 30 to 50 times as much as coal- or nuclear-generated power. The best estimates developed by the Solar Resource Group (1976) for the cost of solar electricity generation by 2010 are $0.042/kWh, whereas conventionally generated power costs only $0.03/kWh. However, the figure of \$0.042/kWh is quite inappropriate as a cost estimate for the extremely complex and cumbersome approaches to solar electricity production using solar thermal techniques now being developed by the U.S. Department of Energy. At best it is an optimistic figure, even for simpler solar electric technologies.

On the other hand, one must be careful not to prejudge the opportunities for innovation. A solar thermal design by Otto Smith of the University of California at Berkeley differs in fundamental ways from those concepts being pursued by the Department of Energy. Professor Smith believes that busbar electricity costs as low as about \$0.036/kWh are feasible, even including enough storage to permit day/night load leveling. Further analysis and testing are clearly in order.

But even to proponents of the wider use of solar energy, solar electricity does not appear to be a feasible competitor to other sources of electricity generation. The only way in which solar electricity could play a significant role by 2010 is through vigorous and massive federal subsidy or through a policy that would not permit development of other generation sources, as in the event of a nuclear moratorium. Nevertheless, widespread interest in solar electric systems will probably encourage the government to build a number of solar thermal plants, virtually regardless of cost.

If photovoltaic devices were to be developed vigorously, they could become important competitors to conventional fuels. Many of the materials, such as silicon, that are sources for photovoltaic devices are intrinsically cheap. The difficulty lies with the processing. There is every possibility that, once major advances occur in solid-state physics, application of those sophisticated techniques will lead to mass production of photovoltaic devices at prices not significantly above the costs of window glass. Indeed, this has reportedly already occurred for the low-efficiency material cadmium sulfide. Thus, innovative research seems required before costs can be lowered. Under these circumstances, the potential impact of photovoltaics seems impossible to assess and certainly defies meaningful economic analysis.

In brief, major allowances for solar electric systems do not now appear appropriate, although because solar thermal electric plants will probably be built, we allow for solar electric systems of all forms to replace 2 quads of primary fossil or nuclear fuel. This would be the equivalent of about 36 gigawatts of conventional generating capacity operating 60 percent of the time (that is, with a 60-percent load factor) and would amount to about 6 percent of installed electricity production in 2010.

In summary, solar energy could produce 6 quads of the energy estimated in the CONAES Demand and Conservation Panel's (1976) scenario B to be required by the buildings sector in 2010. It could replace 8 quads of the energy estimated to be required by the industrial sector and 2 quads as solar electricity. Biomass could replace another 4 quads of energy from nonrenewable sources.

These 20 quads of energy from renewable sources compare favorably with the 1.9 quads from renewable sources estimated by the Demand and Conservation Panel (summarized in Table 5), which is the base case. Table 6 shows the change in the base case with the energy input in the Solar Modification Scenario.

Table 5 Projected 2010 primary energy input in quads, from Demand and Conservation Panel scenario B[a]

Energy source	Use			Total
	Buildings sector	Industrial sector[b]	Transportation sector	
Coal	0.07	26.0	0.2	26.3
Oil	4.8	23.0	25.0	52.8
Gas	5.1	5.7	0.2	11.0
Electricity	26.8	8.9	0.2	35.9
Solar	(0.9)[c]	(1.0)	–	(1.9)
Total[d]	36.8	63.6	25.6	126.0

[a] Primary demand is calculated from end-use demand by converting oil at 1.26 Btu of input per Btu of output energy, gas at 1.16 Btu of input per Btu output, electricity at 3.1 Btu input per Btu output, in accordance with Bureau of Mines convention.

[b] 8.82 quads of agricultural and construction use transferred from buildings sector to industrial (Clark Bullard, U.S. Department of Energy, personal communication).

[c] Solar use is actually greater than figures shown due to use of passive solar design. However, it is impossible to separate passive solar from overall energy-conserving design of building.

[d] Excluding solar

Source: Adapted from Demand and Conservation Panel (1976)

HOW SOON CAN SOLAR TECHNOLOGY BE AVAILABLE?

Plans for introducing any new technology are usually considered in two phases. Start-up time is the year in which commercial prototype units are first installed. The systems constructed may not themselves be economical, but there are sound engineering data to show that, under conditions of mass production, the systems will become economical.

Take-off time is the year in which full-scale commercial production begins. By the time production begins, system reliability has been assured through field testing in the interval since start-up time and

Table 6 Projected 2010 primary energy input in quads, with solar modification[a]

Energy source	Use			Total
	Buildings sector	Industrial sector	Transportation sector	
Coal	0.07	26.0	0.2	26.3
Oil	4.0	16.6	25.0	45.6
Gas	4.3	4.1	0.2	8.6
Electricity	22.4	8.9	0.2	31.5
Solar[b]	(6.0)	(8.0)	–	(14.0)
Total (nonsolar)[c,d]	30.8	55.6	25.6	112.0

[a]Demand and Conservation scenario B'. Primary demand is calculated from end-use demand by converting oil at 1.26 Btu/Btu, gas at 1.16 Btu/Btu, and electricity at 3.1 Btu/Btu, in accordance with Bureau of Mines convention.

[b]Excludes solar electric and biomass. Solar is assumed to displace oil and gas only for process heat.

[c]Solar heating and cooling substitutes virtually interchangeably for all energy forms, according to the Demand and Conservation Panel analysis. In scenario A essentially all of the energy requirements for heating, cooling, and hot water could be replaced by solar (14.6 quads).

[d]Solar electricity (2 quads) and biomass (4 quads) may be allocated arbitrarily among the demand sectors. Biomass replaces gas or oil.

Source: Adapted from Demand and Conservation Panel (1976)

system costs are convincingly known to manufacturers and are competitive with conventional energy forms either because of intrinsically low costs or because of price guarantees, subsidies, or other support.

Table 7 presents estimates of start-up and take-off dates for each major solar technology. These start-up times are believed to be achievable through a vigorous research, development, and demonstration program. The take-off times are the times for critical decision making, and national action may be required to assure that the deadlines are met.

Installed capacity at start-up time is at least 0.03 quad/year, delivered, for solar systems that produce electricity, and 0.1 quad/year

Table 7 Start-up and take-off dates for major solar technologies

Technology	Start-up date	Take-off date
Heating and cooling		
Active	1975	1980
Passive	1960	1975
Biomass	1985	1995
Solar electricity	1985	1995

for other systems. One billion square feet of solar collector corresponds to 0.1 quad capacity per year.

Installed capacity at the time the take-off point is reached is assumed to be 0.5 quad for heating and cooling systems and 0.2 quad to displace primary fuels for central-station electric plants. If the electricity-generating systems were decentralized and used photovoltaic devices, the capacity required would be substantially less.

After take-off time, the various solar technologies are assumed to grow at the rates shown in Table 8. These growth rates will moderate as the market becomes saturated. However, except possibly for domestic and commercial water heating, market saturation is not likely to occur before 2010.

Table 8 Projected growth for solar technologies

Application	Energy produced in quads per year				Growth per year (percent)
	1980	1985	1995	2010	
Industry	0.5			8	12
Heating/cooling		0.5		6	10
Biomass		0.5		4	9
Electricity			0.25	2	15

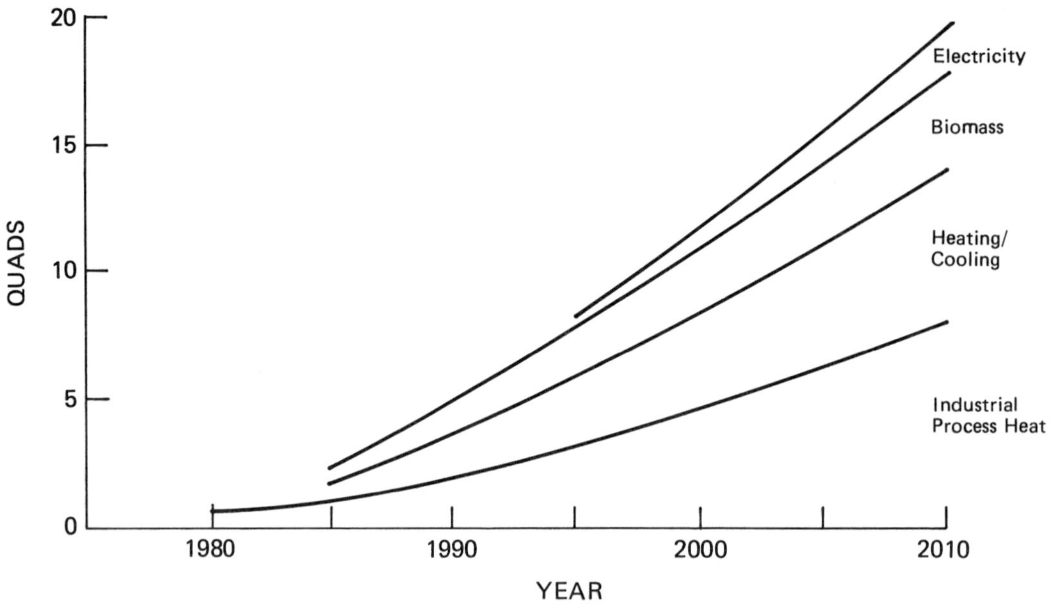

Figure 3 Estimated growth of solar technologies, 1975-2010

The CONAES Modeling Resource Group (National Research Council, 1978) estimated the limit on growth rates for new technologies at 20 percent per year. Our projected growth rates of 10 to 15 percent per year are well below that estimate and are also modest compared with most projected growth rates for nuclear technologies. On the other hand, it is common to delay the introduction of a technology. There can be no question that these growth rates are plausible only if vigorous governmental policy is assumed.

Costs for solar electricity are expected to remain prohibitive at least through 2000, barring a major technological advance. Some solar electric capacity will, however, surely be installed if we are vigorous about developing solar energy. Nevertheless, in contrast with solar heating and cooling and solar process heat, solar electric generation cannot now be considered economically feasible. Subsidies will be needed and are assumed to operate.

It must be recognized that solar energy installations come in many sizes and shapes and have extremely diverse potential. Some of the technologies will surely fail, and others will take forms quite different from those now envisaged. For long-range planning purposes, such shifts have little importance. It is the total impact that matters. Figure 3 illustrates the combined impact of the several solar technologies.

HOW MUCH WOULD SOLAR SYSTEMS COST?

No cost numbers for solar energy systems are credible--at least not within a range that could make decisions on solar and nuclear systems clear and unambiguous. The decisions facing our society as we move from the fossil era to the era of renewable resources transcend cost considerations. Far more important are the implications of the energy systems chosen for availability of energy, social structure, individual freedom, and relations of the United States to the developing nations. It is to these issues rather than to cost that we urge the reader to address her attention as she reads the remainder of this section.

The Solar Resource Group (1976) of CONAES, under the assumption that major research and development programs are successful, estimated that by 2010 costs for delivered solar heat and delivered solar air conditioning (Table 9) will be comparable to or below conventional fuel

Table 9 Delivered solar energy costs in the year 2010

Delivered energy	Cost in dollars per million Btu[a]
Domestic water heat	4.40
Passive space heat	4.60
Active space heat	7.30
Residential air conditioning	19.60 (6.1)
Nonresidential air conditioning	5.00
Process heat	3.76
Bioconversion	0.40-9.00[b]
Electricity	12.40 (4.2)

[a]Cents per kilowatt-hour in parentheses

[b]Depending on source

Source: Adapted from Solar Resource Group (1976)

costs alone for scenario B of the CONAES Demand and Conservation Panel (1976), shown in Table 10.[a]

The argument on behalf of solar energy is even more favorable when equipment costs are taken into account. Thus, from this point of view, a discussion of solar energy's role depends only weakly on economic factors; it depends mainly on market penetration. (The solar electricity situation is a bit different. There are great questions about costs, reliability, and energy-storage technology.)

The point is that, even for sources of supply whose technologies are more or less at hand, the costs of entire systems have not yet been calculated; nor is it usual in energy analyses for such calculations to be made. Government planning documents, such as ERDA-48 (U.S. Energy Research and Development, 1975) and ERDA-76-1 (U.S. Energy Research and Development, 1976), include only costs related to supplying the energy,

Table 10 Energy cost assumptions under Demand and Conservation Panel scenario B, in dollars per million Btu[a]

Energy source	Year			
	2010		1975	
Distillate	6.74		2.81	
Utility residual	4.85		2.02	
Natural gas (total)	7.74		1.29	
Electricity				
Commercial	19.04	(6.50)	9.52	(3.25)
Industrial	10.72	(3.66)	5.36	(1.83)
Residential	18.22	(6.22)	9.11	(3.11)
Demand-weighted average	15.82	(5.40)	7.91	(2.70)

[a]Cents per kilowatt-hour in parentheses

Source: Adapted from Demand and Conservation Panel (1976)

---

[a]The dramatic oil-price increases announced by OPEC in 1979 make near-term solar economics look far better than they did only two years ago, when this report was first drafted.

not those associated with its use. Thus there are estimates of the costs
of generation and transmission systems for electricity but not for the
costs of heat pumps when electricity is to be used for heating.

Such partial analyses of costs, which stop far short of comprehensive systems analyses for these familiar energy sources, would require
expansion to total-cost analyses when systems using solar energy, which
combine investment in conservation with investment in supply and less-
tangible costs for health, aesthetics, and so forth, are being considered.
Indeed, a nationwide analysis of all aspects of the entire energy system,
from source to use, including insulation, lighting levels, heating, ven-
tilating, and air conditioning systems, and others, would necessarily
emphasize energy conservation by focusing attention on the efficiency
of the system as a whole.

Once a comprehensive systems analysis is undertaken, however, the
extent to which solar heating and cooling can cut our use of nonrenewable sources will be apparent. Only then, perhaps, will government planners recognize the contribution possible from solar energy.

In brief, a systems analysis would enable us to see that the efficiency of the system requires us to conserve nonrenewable sources of
energy and thus to turn to renewable sources wherever possible. An economy based on the fullest use of renewable energy would therefore lead us
toward a future in which less energy will be used.

A comprehensive systems analysis will also be favorable to solar
energy from the standpoint of forever reducing our dependence on foreign
oil and foreign fissionable fuel for generating electricity.

One comprehensive set of supply costs has been developed (Lovins,
1976). For example, Lovins finds the total cost of nuclear systems,
taking into account fuel cycle costs, transmission and distribution
costs, and a number of other factors, to be close to $5000 per kilo-
watt of delivered power. This is so much larger than the cost of a
plant alone that further examination is clearly in order. Lovins' summary of the costs of delivered energy using a variety of forms appears
in Table 11.

Investments in energy conservation are frequently far more cost
effective than expenditures on supply expansion. Also, many services
are performed better when energy use is decreased (for example, automobile air pollution is reduced when cars use less gasoline per mile).
Thus it is proper and desirable to associate a renewable-fuel-based
economy with a low-energy future.

There are many reasons why it might be advantageous to use solar
energy even if costs were higher than for conventional systems. Consider electricity. An optimistic busbar cost estimate for solar electricity, including required storage systems, is about $0.045/kWh. This
is about $0.15/kWh greater than current busbar cost estimates for coal-
or nuclear-produced electricity. (Consumer costs for electricity in some
parts of the United States today are running much higher than this--as
much as $0.07/kWh.)[a] The additional annual cost to produce 1.9 trillion

---

[a]These numbers are typical for 1977. Coal-fired plants scheduled to begin
operation in 1985 may produce electricity for as much as $0.08/kWh or more.

Table 11 Capital cost of energy supply and conservation technologies

Technology	Capital cost
	(thousands of dollars per barrel of oil equivalent per day)[a]
Traditional direct fuel technologies, 1950–1970	2–3
Imported oil or domestic coal, 1970s	2–3
Frontier oil and gas, 1980s	10–25[b]
Coal synthetics and exotic hydrocarbons, 1980s	20–40[b]
Central coal-electric with scrubbers, 1980s	170[b]
Light water reactor, mid-1980s	200–300[b]
Fluidized-bed gas turbine/district heating/heat pumps, early 1980s	30[c]
Wind-electric	200[b]
Retrofitted 100% solar space heat, mid 1980s	50–70[c]
Bioconversion of agricultural/forestry residues, 1980s	13–20
Pyrolysis of municipal wastes, late 1970s	30
Improved end-use efficiency	
New commercial buildings	0–3[c]
Common industrial/architectural leak-plugging	0–5[c]
Most industrial/architectural heat-recovery systems	5–15[c]
Difficult, extremely thorough building retrofits	25[c]

[a]1976 dollars

[b]Delivered in the form of electricity

[c]Including cost of end-use devices to deliver desired function

Source: Lovins (1976)

kilowatt-hours of electricity, the amount used in the United States in 1974, is then about $30 billion. This is about half the nation's 1979 total oil import bill.

A national decision to produce 10 percent of this electricity using solar power--which would mean an installed solar capacity equivalent to 38 conventional plants operating at a 60-percent load factor, would carry with it an additional cost of just $16 per person per year.

An even more interesting way to look at an extra cost of solar energy of $0.015/kWh is as an offset to oil imports. The oil-fuel cost corresponding to $0.015/kWh is just $8.80 per barrel (when generation loss is included), which is much less than imported OPEC oil now costs. Thus a premium paid for solar energy can be considered an investment made within the United States to cut back--forever--on oil imports for electricity generation. The investment has a favorable benefit/cost ratio.

In short, although we know less about the costs of entire systems of solar energy than about those of systems using conventional fuels, a comprehensive analysis will prove favorable to solar energy on grounds of conservation, of reducing our dependence on foreign sources of oil and nuclear power, and on the acceptability of the higher cost of a portion of our electricity's being generated by solar energy if nuclear energy and coal are our only alternatives.

ARE THERE NOT GEOGRAPHIC VARIATIONS IN SOLAR ENERGY?

Solar energy varies geographically as well as seasonably, and of course storage must be taken into account when any solar use is being studied. However, solar buildings have been constructed to take maximum advantage of solar energy in Scandinavia, England, and Canada, whose climates are in places far less attractive than any in the United States, and they are proving cost effective. In most parts of the United States, solar hot-water heating and elements of passive design are already cost effective, and this situation will improve as costs of conventional fuels increase and as more experience is gained with solar energy.

CAN SOLAR-ENERGY SYSTEMS AND INSTITUTIONS BE DECENTRALIZED?

Technically there are no compelling reasons to make decentralization of solar energy uses an important issue. Economies of scale in solar technology go both ways. Both the centralized solar electric plant and decentralized heating and cooling have significant roles, and neither excludes the other. Decentralized solar electric power, particularly with advances in storage and photovoltaic techniques, has some advantage from the standpoint of system resiliency. Further research is required. From a technical standpoint, considering factors of economics, system performance, aesthetics, public safety, wartime vulnerability, and multiple use of sunlit areas (as with collectors on rooftops and over highways), applications will arise in which on-site solar technology fits and others in which centralized solar electric technology is better. However, these criteria alone are not likely to decide the outcome. Decisions will be influenced also by the issue of decentralized control.

The symbolic power of the decentralization issue should not be underestimated. Solar energy is democratic; it falls on the rich and the poor, the weak and the powerful. To decentralize solar energy use is to enable individual homes or communities to gather it. The issue of decentralized solar power is symbolic of a greater issue: the preservation of liberty and equity by maintaining some independence from the "big system." As the theorists of free-enterprise democracy considered the principle of control and ownership of property essential to liberty, so the principle of control over indispensable energy supply is now being put forth as a precondition of liberty.

The Symposium on Future Strategies for Energy Development held at Oak Ridge, Tennessee, October 20-21, 1976, brought into sharp focus many of the issues involved in contrasting dispersed technologies with concentrated ones. The arguments for "soft" technologies were presented by Lovins (1976) and those for the capabilities of concentrated technologies by Haefele and Sassin (1976).

Lovins described the philosophy of small-scale systems:

> Some diseconomies of large scale are starting to be widely appreciated. For example, it is now well known that large electrical components, notably turbogenerators, often lose in reliability--hence in contributions to grid operating costs, standby capacity costs, grid instability, and lost revenues--what their size gains in unit capital cost. These effects are so common that there is mounting evidence that most types of power stations can have lower busbar costs in sizes of the order of hundreds rather than of thousands of megawatts.

> Dispersed generation near load centers is well known to improve system integration and stability. According to one recent study . . . it was found that one kilowatt of dispersed generation was equivalent from the standpoint of reserve requirements to 2.5 kilowatts of central generation. The reliability of supply within the network was determined by means of an index related to the LOLP (loss-of-load probability). The reason why the dispersed device can be so effective is that it protects the load in its vicinity against generation _as well as_ transmission and distribution outages. Thus the "dispersion credit" traditionally assigned to local supply--e.g., from battery banks or fuel cells associated with distribution facilities--may be far too low, since it reflects only the cost, on the order of $100/kilowatt, of saved transmission facilities. Unfortunately, publication of a study by the Electric Power Research Institute with this conclusion has been suspended, so few recent data are available. The extreme capital intensity of all electrical facilities offers ample reason to

explore carefully the reliability implications of more centralization. The classical literature of this subject seems
to me sketchy and unpersuasive and its quantification primitive.

A further diseconomy of large scale is so obvious that it
is often forgotten. The past few decades' military experience in Europe and Indochina has taught us that central
energy systems reliant on a few large facilities are far
more vulnerable, and harder to restore when damaged, than
dispersed systems. . . .

Small energy systems suited to particular niches can
mimic the strategy of ecosystem development, adapting and
hybridizing in constant coevolution with a broad front of
technical and social change. Large systems tend to evolve
more linearly like single specialized species (dinosaurs?)
with less genotypic diversity and greater phenotypic fra-
gility. Large systems also accrete costly, specialized
infrastructure that strongly influences future lines of
development. Thus unamortized natural-gas pipelines, the
third largest U.S. industry, provide a strong incentive
to make synthetic pipeline-quality gas even at a price an
order of magnitude higher; building a grid dependent on
1,000-MW blocks of electricity discourages a future shift
to smaller-scale or reduced electrification. Small systems, in contrast, tend to depend more on infrastructure
installed at the point of end use, thus increasing the
user's ability to adapt. For example, resistive heaters
and electric heat pumps are not very adaptable, so an all-
electric house is hard to heat except with electricity
from some source. A domestic or district heating system
based on circulating hot water, however, can use virtually
any heat source at any scale without significant change to
the domestic plumbing, adapting to as wide a range as solar
collectors, solar/heat-pump hybrids, and combined-heat-and-
power district stations. Thus if a transitional technology
such as coal-fired fluidized-bed gas turbines with district
heating is deployed first in those urban areas where solar
backfits will be slowest and least convenient, with district heating clustered in holding tanks of neighborhood
scale, then that interim heat distribution system (coupled
to existing domestic plumbing) can be adapted later to
whatever soft source of heat becomes available in each
neighborhood. Infrastructure at or near the point of end
use can be designed for this sort of piggybacking, whereas
large-scale distribution infrastructure enables one only
to choose one or another kind of enormous central power
station, gas plant, etc.

Haefele and Sassin note that laws of scale tend to drive technologies toward increasingly large units but that on the other hand the

need for redundancy drives in the other direction. For solar systems a major problem is the need for backup systems and for storage, both of which are expensive. Day-to-day energy-storage problems are probably surmountable, but storage to keep pace with seasonal and annual variations is far more difficult to achieve (or requires biomass as the medium of storage). One approach is to disperse the system broadly but to give it the capability to move extremely large amounts of energy from one region to another. A study by R. Partle for the International Institute for Applied Systems Analysis (IIASA), reported by Haefele and Sassin (1976) analyzed movement of 10 gigawatts (electric) over distances of 4000 kilometers, estimating a unit′ cost comparable with that of moving coal by train.

Marchetti (1975) at IIASA has explored the concept of the energy island, which might use breeder reactors at a level of about one terawatt (1000 gigawatts) of thermal energy. This amounts to about 14 percent of the energy used by the entire world today. The concept is intriguing, for it represents an extreme case of decoupling the technology of energy supply from the users of energy. Whether such decoupling could decrease the anxiety associated with large-scale nuclear systems remains uncertain. What is clear, however, is that there are extraordinary choices to be made in terms of energy-system scale and decoupling.

In the final analysis, the issue of large versus small is the issue of coupling people to their energy-supply systems, not an issue of solar power contrasted with nuclear power. Nuclear systems could be made small and used for both district heating and electricity production. Solar systems can be made vast, sited in remote areas with high insolation, and coupled to energy users through massive electrical networks or through other transmission devices, such as liquid nitrogen gas, methanol, or liquid hydrogen tankers.

THE ENERGY POTENTIAL OF SOLAR: OTHER VIEWS

Any attempt to analyze the energy potential of a new technology is fraught with uncertainty and subject to challenge from many fronts. The problem is especially severe in solar energy, for experience to date is so limited and the institutional barriers to success are so great (Schoen, Hirschberg, Weingart, and Stein, 1975). The variations possible are exhibited in the broad range of estimates of solar impacts compiled by the CONAES Solar Resource Group (National Research Council, 1979) and summarized in Table 12.

Clearly, there exists no consensus on how to estimate the potential impact of the solar technologies, even on the assumption of highly competitive prices, when the range of impacts by the year 2000 varies from as low as 1 quad to as high as 94 quads.

Thus the Solar Resource Group estimated the potential for solar heat and electricity. Figure 4 expresses solar-energy contributions as a function of energy cost in 2000. Figure 5 expresses the impact of solar technologies over the period 1975 to 2010 for specified costs of $5/million Btu for heat energy and of 60 mills/kWh for electricity.

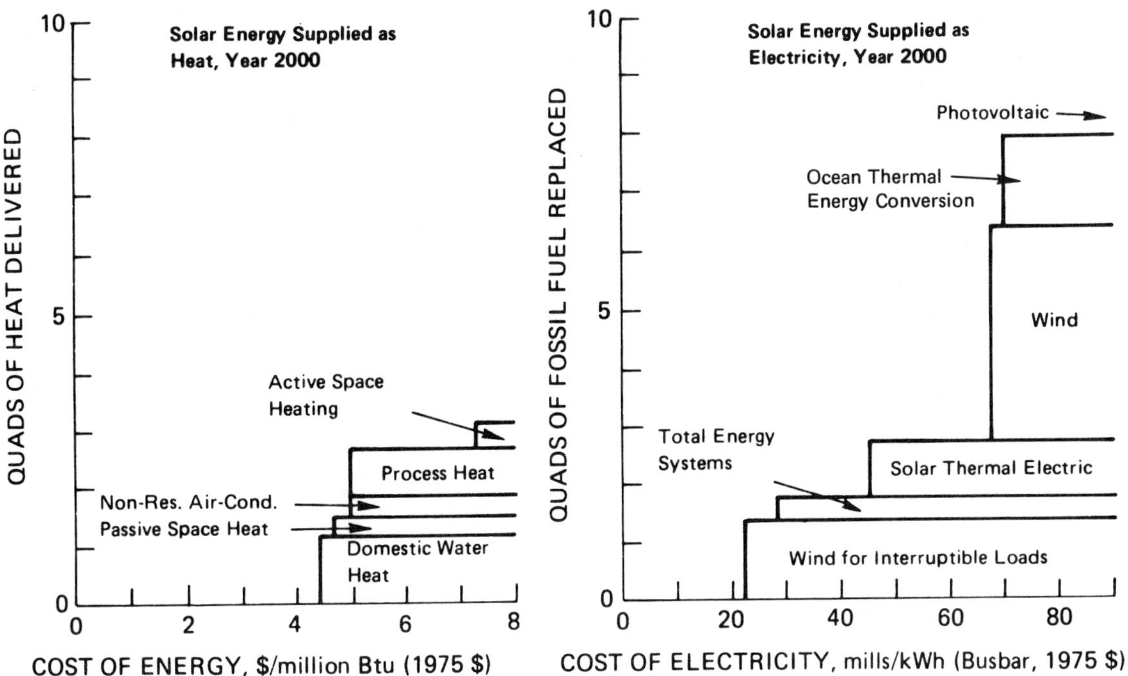

Figure 4   Estimated energy contributions of solar energy technologies
in the year 2000 as a function of costs of competing fuels
(National Research Council, 1979)

The CONAES Demand and Conservation Panel (1976), working in con-
junction with the Solar Resource Group, approached the problem by assuming that solar systems will penetrate the market gradually once they
become competitive. The procedure uses a functional form for the competition, thereby assuring that the new technology occupies its place
gradually. This approach leads to a very low impact in 2010--just 1.9
quads in scenario B. However, by 2010 solar technologies will begin to
have a fairly rapid impact. Figure 6 portrays the impact of one kind
of solar technology: residential space heating.

Another approach to estimating the impact of solar energy is suggested by Lovins (1976), who analyzes energy use in terms of the required
thermodynamic quality of the energy. His approximate analysis for Canada
is shown in Fig. 7. The figure compares 1973 end uses with 2025 end uses

Table 12 Forecasts of solar energy applications in the year 2000, in quads

Source	Date	Solar thermal and photovoltaic	Wind and ocean thermal energy conversion	Other solar	Total
Donovan et al.[a]	Dec 72	3.1	2.4	6.5	12.0
NASA/ASEE[b]	Sept 73	0	0	3.5-6.1	3.5-6.1
Solar hearings[c]	Nov 73	5.3	15	4.5	24.8
MITRE[d]	Nov 73	7-18	11-27	18	36-63
Council on Environmental Quality[e]	Mar 74	0	0	1	1
Ford Foundation[f]	Late 74	1	1	2	4
Federal Energy Administration[g]	Nov 74	6-27	19-40	8-27	34-94
Teller[h]	April 75	0	0	5	5
ERDA-48[i]	June 75	1.3-6.1	0	5	6.3-11.1
ERDA-49[j]	June 75	3.1	1.8	6	10.9
Candela and Wiener[k]	Aug 75	6-9	6-9	6-9	18-27

[a]Donovan, P. I., W. Woodward, W. R. Cherry, F. A. Morse, and L. O. Herwig. 1972. An Assessment of Solar Energy as a National Energy Resource. Springfield, Va.: National Technical Information Service (PB-221659)

[b] National Aeronautics and Space Administration and American Society of Electrical Engineers System Design Summer Faculty Program. 1973. TERRASTAR: Terrestrial Applications of Solar Technology and Research, Final Report. Springfield, Va.: National Technical Information Service (N-74-12674).

[c] U.S. House of Representatives. 1974. Hearings on the Solar Energy Research, Development, and Demonstration Act, H.R. 10952. Subcommittee on Energy, Committee on Science and Astronautics. 93rd Congress, 1st session, Washington, D.C.: U.S. Government Printing Office.

[d] MITRE Corporation. 1973. Systems Analysis of Solar Energy Programs. McLean, Va.: MITRE Corporation (MTR-6513).

[e] U.S. Council on Environmental Quality. 1974. A National Energy Conservation Program: The Half and Half Plan. Washington, D.C.: U.S. Government Printing Office.

[f] Ford Foundation. 1974. A Time to Choose: America's Energy Future. Final Report by the Energy Policy Project of the Ford Foundation. Cambridge, Mass.: Ballinger.

[g] Federal Energy Administration. 1974. Project Independence Blueprint, Final Task Force Report: Solar Energy. Springfield, Va.: National Technical Information Service (PB-248507).

[h] Teller, E. 1975. Energy: A Plan for Action. Report to the Energy Panel of the Commission on Critical Choices for Americans. New York: The Third Century Corporation.

[i] U.S. Energy Research and Development Administration. 1975a. A National Plan for Energy Research, Development and Demonstration. Washington, D.C.: U.S. Energy Research and Development Administration (ERDA 48).

[j] U.S. Energy Research and Development Administration. 1975b. National Solar Energy Research, Development and Demonstration Program: Definition Report. Washington, D.C.: U.S. Energy Research and Development Administration (ERDA 49).

[k] Candela, B. J., and A. J. Wiener. 1975. Lifestyle and Energy Consumption: Scenarios for the Years 1985, 2000, and 2025--Alternative Coal Futures in the American Economy. Task 5 of Issues Relative to the Development and Commercialization of a Coal-Derived Synthetic Liquids Industry. Springfield, Va.: National Technical Information Service (FE-1752-1).

Source: National Research Council (1979)

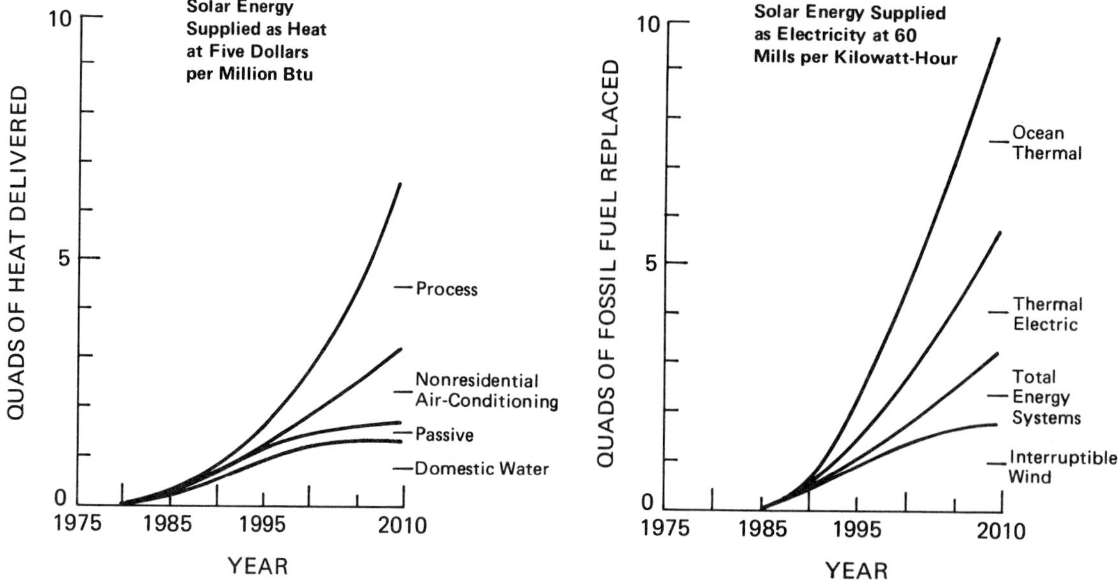

Figure 5 Estimated increases in energy contributions of solar energy
technologies used to supply heat at less than five dollars
per million Btu or electricity at less than 60 mills per
kilowatt-hour in the year 2000 (Solar Resource Group, 1976)

when energy is supplied by a "super-technical fix" and, alternatively,
by a "soft" source. The "soft" energy mix uses solar energy for virtually all low-temperature heat and would thus provide about one-third of
the total energy input to the Canadian system. There is no allowance
for solar electricity.

Finally, the United States government's approach has been to emphasize solar electricity rather than other forms of solar energy. The
President's budget to Congress for fiscal 1977 included $102 million for
solar electric research out of a total request of $160 million for solar
energy. Congress acted by appropriating $174.9 million for solar elec-
tric energy and $290.4 million for all solar research and development.
The Department of Energy continues to emphasize solar electricity, though
less than in years past. Most estimates of the costs of generating electricity by solar energy are considerably higher than the costs associated
with conventional coal-fired or nuclear-fired generating systems.

Until recently, solar energy and renewable technologies have not
received serious government attention. In part as a result of citizen
action, this situation has changed strikingly in recent years, as is
evident in the budget for solar research and development. The federal
budget has grown exponentially for several years, with a doubling time
of less than a year (Fig. 8).

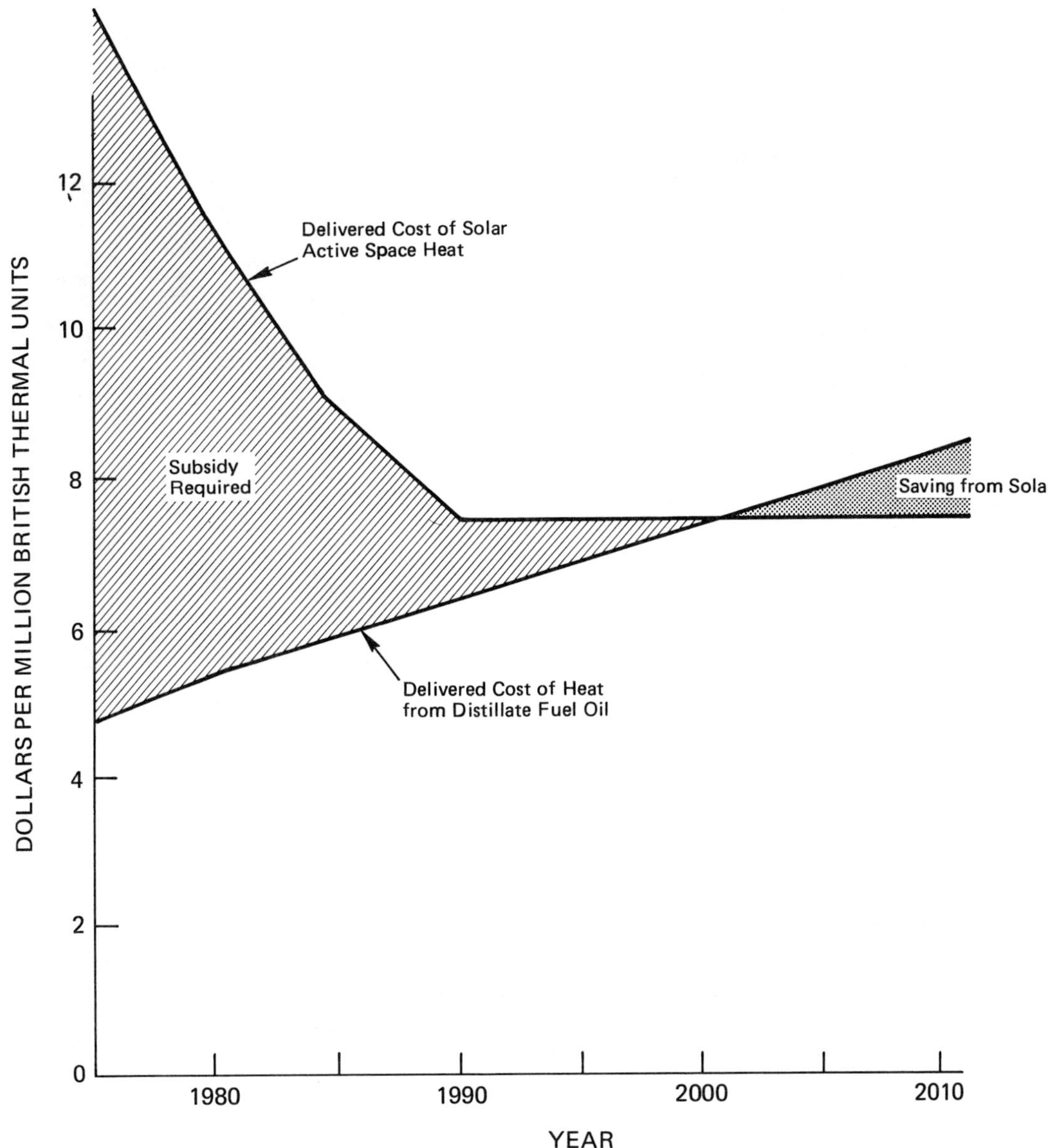

Figure 6 Estimated cost impact of solar technology on residential space heating

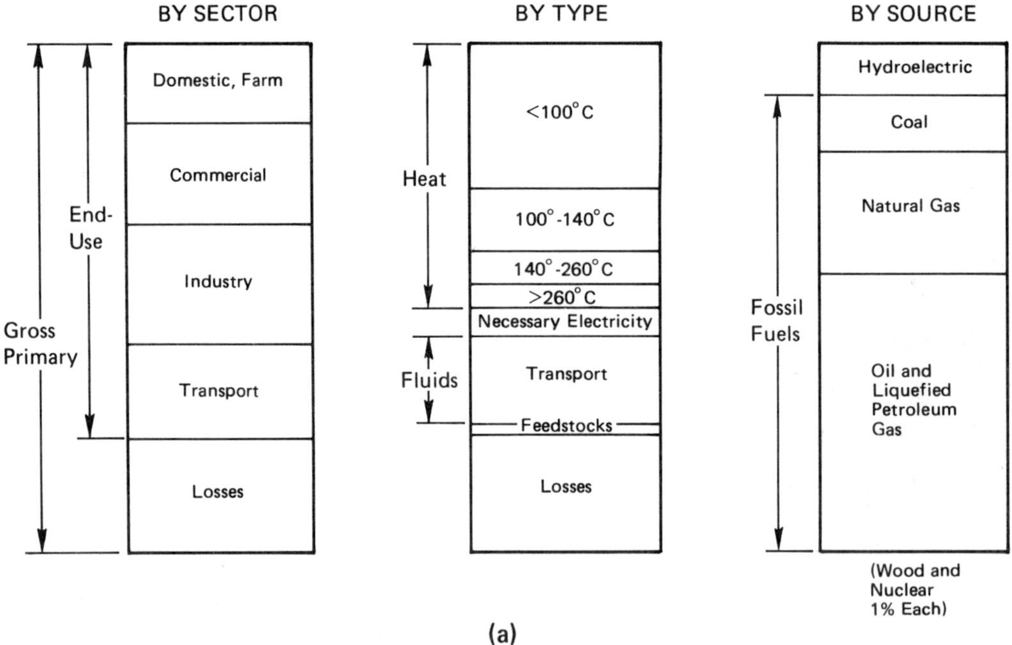

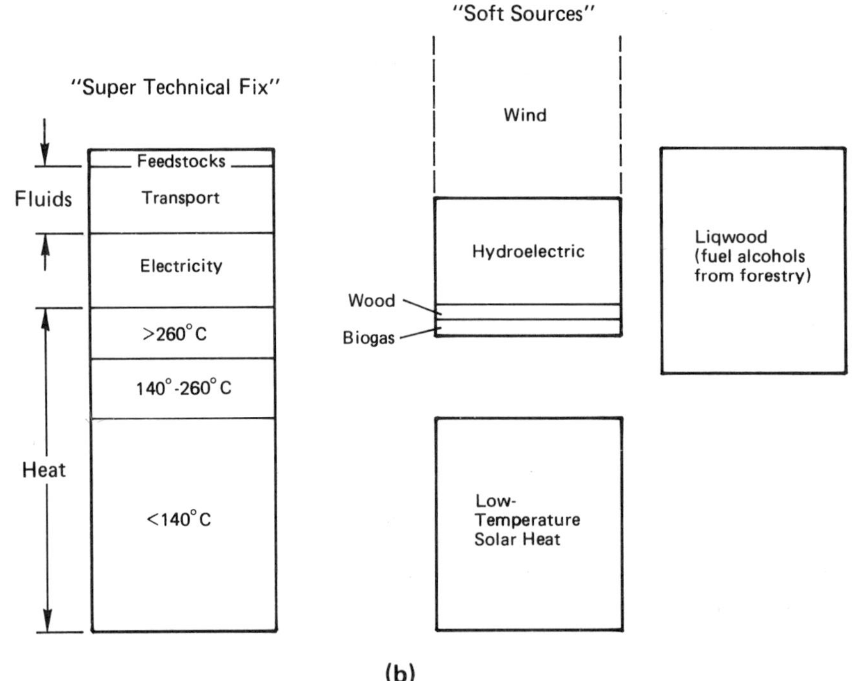

Figure 7   Canadian energy use:
(a) in 1973 (total 6.6 quads, population 22 million) and
(b) in 2025 (total 5.9 quads, population 40 million), as
projected by assuming (left) "super technical fix" and
(right) "soft" sources (Adapted from Lovins, 1976)

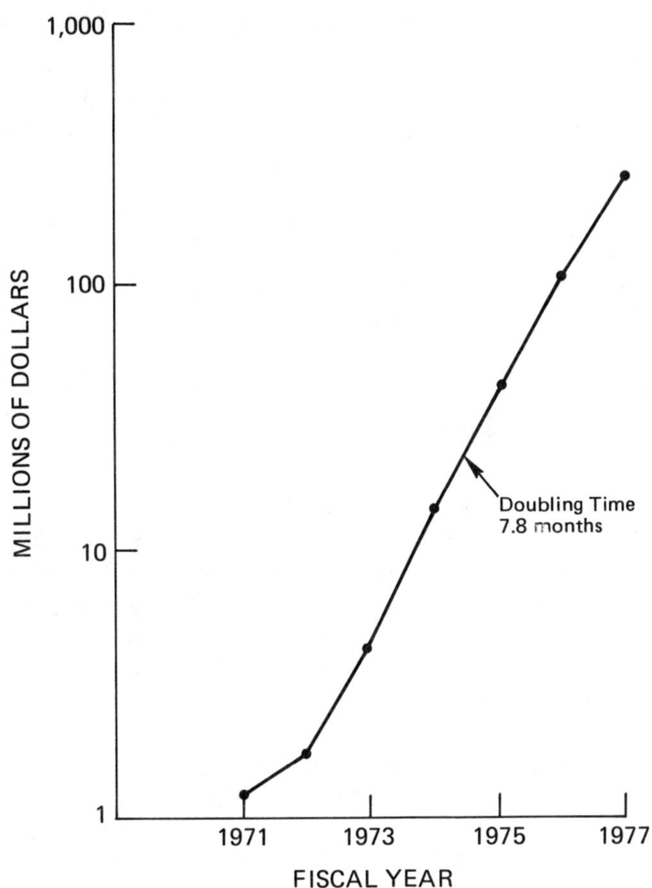

Figure 8   Federal budget authority for solar energy research and
development funded by the National Science Foundation up to
1975 and the Energy Research and Development Administration
from 1975 to 1977 (Solar Resource Group, 1976)

Yet, for what needs to be done, this budget is small, and its emphasis on solar electricity is almost perverse. On the face of it, a
national decision to "go solar" seems unlikely.

    There is, however, at least one precedent from the recent past in
which the direction of government action was decisively reoriented.
The environmental legislation of the late 1960's and early 1970's was
enacted through pressure brought by a coalition of interest groups having
diverse beliefs. Some of the factors that could motivate the formation
of a coalition capable of rapidly shifting governmental emphasis to renewable forms of energy are the following:

   ● <u>Climatic Modifications</u>. At present, there is growing evidence
      for the view that release of carbon dioxide or particulates
      into the atmosphere will have a long-term impact on global

climate. As analytic techniques improve, a consensus may develop among scientists concerning the likelihood of major climatic modifications if fossil fuels continue to be used. Such a consensus could lead to decisions to deemphasize their use.

- <u>Nuclear Accidents, Diversion, Waste Management</u>. Major nuclear accidents in the United States or elsewhere could lead to international reaction against any large-scale implementation of nuclear power.

- <u>Environmental Sensitivity</u>. Within the past few years many laws have been passed in the United States and elsewhere encouraging preservation of the environment.

Our assessment of the energy potential of solar technologies is optimistic but credible. Because of the constraints on the development of alternative energy technologies discussed above, public speculation on the long-term social implications of solar energy remains, for the most part, incomplete. Solar-powered devices and techniques--in part because they are still novel--attract large audiences. But then, the adoption of new ideas and products has always been part of the American tradition. Witness the success of electronic calculators, which made mechanical calculators obsolete almost overnight.

We assume that the American people and the government officials representing them will respond pragmatically to the present challenge. The combination of public opinion and shifting priorities on renewable forms of energy in government energy policies could stimulate action in the following ways: the sharp rise in energy prices could encourage investment in solar energy earlier than might be expected on economic grounds; the specter of energy shortages could encourage a rapid transition to renewable resources; governmental incentives, such as tax deductions, could encourage renewable technologies; and changes in values that emphasize scarcity, thrift, simplicity, or survival could discourage continuing use of conventional energy forms, despite their advantageous costs, for purposes such as generating electricity.

REFERENCES

Demand and Conservation Panel. 1976. Draft report to the Committee on
Nuclear and Alternative Energy Systems, National Research Council,
Washington, D.C. December.

Dow Chemical Co. 1975. Evaluation of New Energy Sources for Process
Heat. Prepared for the National Science Foundation. Midland, Mich.:
Dow Chemical Co.

Haefele, W., and W. Sassin. 1976. Contrasting Views of the Future and
Their Influence on our Technological Horizons for Energy. In Future
Strategies for Energy Development: A Question of Scale. Oak Ridge,
Tenn.: Oak Ridge Associated Universities.

Hubbert, M. K. 1974. U.S. Energy Resources: A Review as of 1972,
Pt. 1. In A National Fuels and Energy Policy Study. U.S. Congress,
Senate, Committee on Interior and Insular Affairs. Serial No. 93-40
(92-75). Washington, D.C.: U.S. Government Printing Office.

Lovins, A. 1976. Scale, Centralization and Electrification in Energy
Systems. In Future Strategies for Energy Development: A Question of
Scale. Oak Ridge, Tenn.: Oak Ridge Associated Universities.

Marchetti, C. 1975. Geoengineering and the Energy Island. Second
Status Report of the IIASA Project on Energy Systems. Laxenberg,
Austria: International Institute for Applied Systems Analysis
(RR-76-1).

National Research Council. 1978. Energy Modeling for an Uncertain
Future. Modeling Resource Group, Synthesis Panel, Committee on
Nuclear and Alternative Energy Systems. Washington, D.C.: National
Academy of Sciences.

National Research Council. 1979. Domestic Potential of Solar and
Other Renewable Energy Sources. Solar Resource Group, Supply and
Delivery Panel, Committee on Nuclear and Alternative Energy Systems.
Washington, D.C.: National Academy of Sciences.

Schoen, R., A. S. Hirschberg, J. M. Weingart, and J. Stein. 1975.
New Energy Technology for Buildings. Cambridge, Mass.: Ballinger.

Solar Resource Group. 1976. Draft report to the Supply and Delivery
Panel, Committee on Nuclear and Alternative Energy Systems, National
Research Council, Washington, D.C. August 9.

Stanford Research Institute. 1976. A Preliminary Social and
Environmental Assessment of the ERDA Solar Program 1975-2020. Draft D
Final Report, July. Menlo Park, Calif.: Stanford Research Institute.

Unger, Samuel G. 1975. Energy Utilization in the Leading Energy-Consuming Food Processing Industries. Food Technology 29(December): 33-46.

U.S. Energy Research and Development Administration. 1975. A National Plan for Energy Research, Development and Demonstration. Washington, D.C.: U.S. Government Printing Office (ERDA-48).

U.S. Energy Research and Development Administration. 1976. A National Plan for Energy Research, Development and Demonstration: Creating Energy Choices for the Future. Washington, D.C.: U.S. Government Printing Office (ERDA-76-1).

Workshop on Alternative Energy Strategies. 1976. Energy Demand Studies: Major Consuming Countries. Cambridge, Mass.: MIT Press.

5 A HIGH–ENERGY–PRODUCTIVITY SOCIETY:

CONSERVATION AND EFFICIENCIES

This scenario is not presented as a prediction of what will happen but
is intended to explore the questions: What would life be like in the
United States in 2010 if, instead of increasing the total consumption
of energy, we consumed approximately the same amount? Would major lifestyle changes be required for such a situation, or would only some rather
insignificant behavioral changes be required of society? Does a significant reduction in per-capita energy use necessitate a lower overall
standard of living?

In this scenario, as in others prepared for this study, a 35-percent
increase in the U.S. population, stabilizing at about 280 million in
2010, is assumed. During this period, it is assumed that prices for
energy will quadruple (relative to those for other commodities), the GNP
will increase at an annual rate of 1 percent per capita per year, and
government's share of personal income will remain relatively constant.
Finally, it is assumed that the United States economic system will
remain essentially unchanged. That is, it will continue to be fundamentally a market economy with considerable individual freedom in the dis-
position of personal income.

This scenario assumes that higher energy costs will become the primary impetus for society to choose behavioral patterns and technologies
that result in a 72-quad national energy economy. It differs in an
important way from the other scenario presented here (Chapter 6), in
that it does not depend on any substantial change in dominant societal
values or lifestyle patterns. It does assume significant increases in
the efficiency with which energy is used (achievable with known technologies), as well as minor changes in living and working patterns. The
assumed behavioral patterns are not alien to this country. In fact, they
are characteristic of some families and some commercial operations now.

SETTING OF THE PROBLEM

From 1950 to 1970, U.S. energy consumption and GNP grew together. These
data are the basis for the argument that there is, and will be, a relatively fixed relationship between total energy use and economic product.
Such interpretations of available data elicit beliefs that, if energy
consumption were reduced, GNP would decline, lowering the standard of
living and resulting in unacceptable lifestyle changes. Because of this
widely held belief, the following question is explored: Can a plausible
scenario for 2010 be envisioned for which explicitly assumed behavioral
and technological changes result in reduced energy consumption and increased per-capita income?

To approach this question, a discussion of past and present data on
consumer expenditures is in order (Bureau of the Census, 1975a, 1975b;
Bureau of Economic Analysis, 1976; Kravis et al., 1975). Table 13 dis-
plays a breakdown into five categories of the GNP in the United States
over time. Since 1941, the major components of the GNP have approximately maintained their relative positions as a proportion of total GNP.
In descending order, these components are: services, nondurable goods,
durable goods other than structures, structures, and energy goods and
services. Table 14 shows personal consumption expenditures in somewhat
more detail (10 categories). Although there have been no drastic changes
since 1945, some trends are observable. Relative expenditures for food

Table 13 Components of gross national product in billions of 1972
dollars per year

Component	Year				
	1929	1941	1950	1960	1973
Structures	41	41	66	88	140
Other durable goods	33	43	65	89	191
Nondurable goods	98	131	163	199	300
Services	109	159	186	295	481
Energy goods and services	25	30	53	69	121

Source: Nordhaus (1976a)

Table 14 Personal consumption expenditures, 1945–1970, in percent per year

Type of product	Year				
	1945	1950	1960	1965	1970
Food, beverages, and tobacco	36.4	30.4	26.9	24.8	23.2
Clothing, accessories, and jewelry	16.4	12.4	10.2	10.0	10.0
Personal care	1.7	1.3	1.6	1.8	1.7
Housing	10.4	11.1	14.2	14.7	14.7
Household operation	13.0	15.4	14.4	14.3	14.0
Medical care	4.2	4.6	5.9	6.5	7.6
Personal business	3.9	3.6	4.6	5.1	5.7
Transportation	5.7	12.9	13.3	13.4	12.6
Recreation	5.1	5.8	5.6	6.1	6.5
Other	3.2	2.4	3.3	3.5	3.9
Total[a]	100.0	100.0	100.0	100.0	100.0

[a]Details may not add due to rounding.

Source: Nordhaus (1976a)

and clothing have declined while those for housing and medical care
have risen. The percentage of total expenditures allocated for transportation more than doubled shortly after World War II and then leveled
off. This change is attributed primarily to increased incomes, which
led to purchases of single family homes in the suburbs, increasing
travel requirements for work, shopping, and schooling; the increase in
income also permitted more travel for recreation.

In terms of energy intensities, the picture since World War II is
mixed. Transportation is energy intensive, whereas medical care and
personal business (insurance, financial services) are relatively low in

energy intensity. Clothing and food, for which percentage expenditures decreased over time, are in between. (Note that these intensity estimates are historically based and do not reflect potential energy savings from behavioral or technological changes.)

Given the above assumptions regarding population, GNP, and energy-price increases, what set of consumer responses might be undertaken to change the overall consumption pattern so as to maintain current levels of energy use until the year 2010? The assumed quadrupling of energy prices relative to other economic goods results in the latter's being substituted for energy, and tends to reduce the consumption of energy-intensive goods and services (e.g., space heat or plastic cups). To reduce building-energy consumption, indoor use of sweaters in winter or reliance on natural ventilation instead of air conditioning in summer are obvious substitutions. The substitution of public for private transportation is one means of reducing gasoline consumption. Consumers may also reduce their total distance traveled or lower energy consumption in the home by changing their thermostat settings.

Manufacturers, especially those requiring significant energy inputs to their production processes, will also be inclined to reduce energy use from economic considerations. New industrial plants may also contribute to these savings if the savings potential is large; the most energy-efficient technologies could be directly implemented without losses incurred from prematurely retiring existing equipment. In existing plants, installing new conserving technologies and improving housekeeping practices generally can produce somewhat smaller savings. Owners of commercial establishments should be expected to respond similarly.

Countering this energy-conserving behavior is the assumed rise in real per-capita income, which allows consumers to spend more on all goods and services, including energy. However, the expected net effect is a reduction in per-capita energy use because the 42-percent increase in GNP is proportionately much smaller than the 400-percent energy-price increase. If energy consumption did not decrease, the proportion of disposable income spent for energy goods and services would rise dramatically, at the expense of other purchases.

The energy-price increases assumed imply an increase in the flow of energy-related information to both producers and consumers. Both groups will be induced to learn how to save energy. Life-cycle costing concepts are expected to become more widely used by both consumers and producers in their decision processes. For example, producers should be more likely to manufacture energy-efficient appliances and publicize this efficiency to potential consumers.

The next section quantifies the effects on household energy consumption resulting from specific behavioral and technological changes. These changes are indicative of responses to increased relative energy prices and to legislation intended to dampen energy-demand growth.

The section that follows presents similar analyses for behavioral and technological changes to reduce the energy demand for transportation. The primary focus is on changes involving residential heating, cooling, water heating, and transportation because energy is consumed directly for these functions and because consumers can, to a considerable extent, regulate their level of consumption.

The next section presents a detailed scenario quantifying energy use by function for a hypothetical 72-quad U.S. energy demand in the year 2010. The scenario incorporates the material on energy conservation potential presented in the previous sections, as well as analyses of energy-conservation measures applicable to production in the industrial sector; the latter information is presented in the footnotes to Table 22.

The final section sketches how such a scenario might be implemented. Detailed qualitative analyses of implementation tools and their impacts are given for some of the measures.

The analysis presented is only partial because of the complexities involved in technological and behavioral changes and because only one resource (energy) is singled out for attention. Energy savings can be achieved, but the implications of these savings in terms of the expenditures of other scarce resources (for example, water) have not been estimated. Ideally, all resource requirements should be considered simultaneously, because saving one resource at the expense of another may not be prudent.

ENERGY SAVINGS IN RESIDENTIAL BUILDINGS

The 1976 levels of energy use in residential buildings (by housing type and end use) are given in Table 15. Estimated energy savings for a number of technological and behavioral changes are given in Tables 16 (cooling) and 17 (heating). The estimates are drawn from the Buildings chapters of the CONAES Demand and Conservation Panel (1976) report. Possible energy reductions for heating water are given in Tables 18 (conventional systems) and 19 (solar systems), based on work performed at the Lawrence Berkeley Laboratory.

ENERGY SAVINGS IN TRANSPORTATION

Table 20 gives a breakdown of passenger trips made by private car during 1969 and 1970. Although the activities are loosely classified, one should note that only a small fraction of all miles driven are for vacation or for recreational purposes. Most trips are made to accomplish specific tasks, such as travel to work or to shop.

Columns in Table 20 give (by trip type) the percentage of total trips, the percentage of total miles driven, the average trip length, the load factor (persons per vehicle), the fuel economy relative to a warmed-up vehicle, and the percentage of total gasoline consumed. The relative economy was derived from calculations of trip length and effective fuel economy made by Austin and Hellman (1975). Fuel economy depends strongly on whether the automobile is warmed up; the reference cited gives reasonable figures for actual fuel economy relative to the fuel economy achieved after 40 miles of relatively stop-free driving. Their calculations also take into account stops and to some extent traffic congestion. The most dramatic finding is that, although trips of under

Table 15   1976 energy end use in quads[a] in residential buildings

Energy use	Single family house	Multi-family house	Mobile home
Space heating	7.24	1.39	0.30
Water heating	1.58	0.65	0.12
Refrigeration	0.90	0.40	0.06
Cooking	0.56	0.22	0.03
Air conditioning	0.98	0.18	0.04
Other	1.48	0.67	0.09
Total	12.74	3.51	0.64
Units of housing stock (millions)	48.3	21.5	3.0
Average energy consumption per unit (10^8 Btu)	2.6	1.6	2.1

[a]Unless otherwise specified

Source: Adapted from Demand and Conservation Panel (1976)

1.5 miles constitute only about 3 percent of all miles driven, they consume nearly 12 percent of all fuel. Reducing total miles driven saves most fuel if the number of shorter trips is reduced.

Table 21 gives estimates of the percentage of vehicle miles in each class and overall and the percentage of gasoline that would be saved if specific changes in automobile use actually occurred. The Austin-Hellman relative fuel economy results generally hold for all kinds and sizes of vehicles. (These results do not hold for diesel automobiles, which perform better than conventional cars in congested or slow traffic relative to fully warmed-up highway use, or for electric vehicles, which require no warming up and do not idle, thus eliminating the major losses of fuel in shorter, intra-city trips. However, it is assumed that the impact of either diesel cars or electric cars will be less than the potential impact of changed driving habits in conventional cars.) There are cars now on the road that average 44 miles per gallon (mpg) in city traffic and 52 mpg on the highway. Should diesel vehicles become common, the fleet average fuel economy would, of course, improve. To account for

Table 16 Actions to reduce space-cooling requirements in residential
units

Actions	Savings (percent)	Comments
Increase thermostat setting	8% per degree F raised	Highly variable, depending on location;
Open windows to cool when possible	12 to 73	Lower savings in more extreme climates[a]
Use window unit to cool X% of house instead of cooling all of house with central unit	100-X	Window units are usually more efficient; therefore this is probably a conservative estimate.
Install a high-efficiency window unit instead of an average window unit	Up to 50	Using currently marketed air conditioners

[a]Pilati (1976)

Source: Adapted from National Research Council (1979)

improved fuel efficiency of conventional gasoline-powered vehicles, conservative figures (considerably lower fuel economy than technically possible) of 25 mpg (city) and 35 mpg (highway) are assumed and then applied to driving-habit savings for these vehicles. The relative savings made by changing driving habits and lifestyles are multiplied by the overall reduction in fuel intensity (gallons/mile) offered by more-energy-efficient vehicles.

The tables illustrating the nature of reduced driving and resulting gasoline use are for discussion purposes only. They are illustrative and not predictive. We do not know the gasoline price required to bring about the changes discussed, nor can we predict how cities might be designed to reduce the need for travel except to say that more compact cities decrease the need for travel, especially travel to work.

AN ENERGY-CONSUMPTION SCENARIO FOR 2010

The two previous sections presented estimates of the energy-saving potential from a variety of behavioral and technological changes. Table 22 combines the impacts of a number of assumed changes to give a detailed

Table 17 Actions to reduce space-heating requirements in residential units

Action	Percentage of space heating energy saved	Comments
Lower thermostat setting	5.5% per degree F lowered	Average within normal range of human comfort. Population-weighted U.S. average. (Pilati, 1976)
Reduce thermostat from 72°F to 68°F day, 55°F night (10 pm to 6 am)	37	Population-weighted U.S. average. (Pilati, 1976)
Heat only part of house (both day and night)	71% in unheated portion of house	Assumes unheated portion of house is at 55°. 71% based on conservative extrapolations.
Install an electric heat pump instead of electric resistance heater	50	Applicable only if electric resistance heat is the alternative; large savings possible because electric resistance is most inefficient overall.
Reduce house size per capita	Same percentage as reduction in floor space	A rough approximation.
Construct houses out of 2" x 6" exterior walls instead of 2" x 4" walls	65	See National Research Council (1979) for information on insulation measures included in this calculation.

Construct houses out of double 2" x 4" exterior walls, having south-facing windows	82	See National Research Council (1979) for more information.
Retrofit houses with more ceiling insulation, weather stripping, storm windows, wall insulation; about 50% of present stock can be retrofitted	50	Using separate numbers below: For windows, walls, and ceilings, 46%; additional 4% for caulking and weather stripping assumed; conservative assumption.
Insulate ducting in forced air systems	20	Hise and Holman (1975).
Retrofit storm windows only	21	Moyers (1971).
Add 6" ceiling insulation	15	Moyers (1971).
Insulate walls	19	Moyers (1971).
Install more efficient gas or oil furnace	Up to 35	Higher savings possible with a gas heat pump.

Source: Adapted from Pilati (1976). Used with permission from _Energy_, vol. 1, "Residential Energy Savings through Modified Control of Space-conditioning Equipment," copyright Pergamon Press, Ltd.

Table 18   Energy saving changes in water heating systems

Action	Energy saved, in percent
Insulate heater with 4-5 inch insulation	9
Reduce use to 40 gallons per day by using flow restrictors, warm water for dishwashing and clothes washing, care taken with all water use	12.5
Reduce temperature and assume 62 gallons used at 120° F instead of 50 gallons at 140° F	16.5
Combination of three above actions	30

[a]All figures based on calculations made at Lawrence Berkeley Laboratory with the standby losses of the A. O. Smith water heater. The losses are consistent with Quinn (1972). We assume a 30-gallon water heater and 50 gallons per day use at 140° F for a household of three.

Table 19   Energy savings in water heating through use of solar energy[a]

Action	Energy saved, in percent
Install solar water heaters	50
Reduce temperature to 120° F and reduce use to 40 gallons per day	30
Combine two actions above	65

[a]Based on calculations made at Lawrence Berkeley Laboratory

Table 20   Automobile use by trip, purpose, length and fuel use

Purpose of trip	Percentage of all trips[a]	Percentage of total vehicle miles traveled[a]	Average length of trip (miles)[a]	Load factor	Relative fuel economy[b]	Percentage of total fuel use
Work						
Commute[c]	32.3	34.1	9.4	1.4	0.75	34.1
Business-related	4.4	8.0	16.1	1.4	0.85	7.1
Total	36.7	42.1	10.2[d]	1.4[d]	0.8[d]	41.2
Family business[c]						
Medical	1.7	1.6	8.4			
Shopping	15.4	7.6	4.4	2.0	0.65	22.7
Other	14.1	10.3	6.5			
Total	31.2	19.5	5.6[d]	2.0		
Education, civic, religious	9.4	5.0	4.7	2.5	0.60	5.8
Social						
Vacation	0.1	2.6	160.0	3.3	1.0	2.0
Visit	9.1	12.2	12.0	2.5	0.8	11.5
Pleasure	1.4	3.1	20.0	2.5	0.9	2.6
Other[e]	12.0	15.4	11.4	2.5	0.8	14.4
Total	22.6	33.3	13.1[d]	2.5[d]	0.87[d]	30.5

[a]Adapted from U.S. Federal Highway Administration (1969)
[b]Austin and Hellman (1975)
[c]Half of all commute trips and 75% of all family business trips less than five miles
[d]Weighted average
[e]Includes recreation and entertainment

Table 21 Potential reduction in miles traveled and gasoline use, compared to 1970

Automobile use	Reduction in total vehicle miles traveled (percent)	Reduction in fuel use (percent)		
		Using 13.7- mpg car	Using 25- mpg car	Using 35- mpg car
Work				
Increase load factor in commute to 2[a]	17.0	16.4	24.7	27.2
Decrease business miles 20%	1.6	1.4	4.0	4.9
Family business-- 50% reduction in trips[b]	7.8	11.8	16.7	18.4
Civic, education, religious	0	0	2.6	3.5
Social				
Vacation[c]	0.5	0.4	0.9	1.2
Visits[d]	0	0	5.2	7.0
Pleasure[d]	1.6	1.3	1.9	2.1
Other[d]	5.3	5.8	9.2	10.7
Total savings	33.8	37.1	65.2	75.0

[a]Trips 5% longer to account for pick-up and drop-off

[b]Average number of trips per day reduced by half; average distance per trip increased by 20%

[c]Vacation is 20% closer to home or eliminated

[d]Shorter trips walked or eliminated; average trip length increased

energy-consumption scenario for 2010. Estimates of the energy saving
potential are discussed in the footnotes to Table 22, in the appendix
to this chapter.

In Table 22, the first column gives 1972 energy consumption by end
use. (More recent data indicate that energy consumption in 1975 was
quite similar to that in 1972.) The energy-saving potentials for each
technological and behavioral option adopted, given as percentages of
1972 consumption, are shown in the second column. Current energy consumption is multiplied by one hundred minus the potential energy saving
percentage, and then divided by 1972 population (207 million people) to
yield potential energy consumption per capita (or per household, where
applicable) for each activity, if the conservation measures were uni-
formly implemented. This result is then scaled up or down depending on
the relative per-capita activity level (2010 versus today), shown in
column 3. This activity-level factor attempts to account for the effects
of rising per-capita income and saturation of each energy-consuming end
use. Finally, the projected population estimate for 2010 of 278.8 million
people is used to scale up per-capita energy use in calculating the total
energy consumption by end use for 2010, given in the fourth column.
Footnotes, in column 5, refer to the appendix, where specific conservation measures that could bring about the energy saving for each end use
are indicated.

Although energy-price responses are not directly modeled, they are
incorporated in the calculations through the saving factors. The estimates in Table 22 agree closely with those of the Demand and Conservation
Panel (1976). In the residential sector, the Demand and Conservation
Panel results are based on an engineering-economic model in which energy
prices are included. In the commercial sector, roughly estimated overall
efficiencies for each building type were assumed. The industrial-sector
results are also based on judgmental actions expected to take place if
energy prices quadruple. Energy savings in the transportation sector
are assumed to result from increased energy prices in the case of the
behavioral changes and from higher efficiency standards in the case of
the technological changes. The standards and/or technological changes
may also arise from higher energy prices. For a complete description
of sectoral responses, see Demand and Conservation Panel (1976).

A summary of the estimates presented in Table 22 is given in
Table 23.

The overall conclusion is that, without any drastic reorganization
of living, working, and transportation patterns, per-capita energy consumption can be lowered. In the face of a population increase of 35
percent between 1972 and 2010, the postulated set of behavioral and technical changes results in only a 2-percent increase in energy consumption.
Per-capita energy consumption decreases by 24 percent.[a]

---

[a]An analysis of the energy-conservation potential for California with
similar input data and assumptions (although with a considerably more
detailed treatment of the growth and decay of energy using stocks and
calculation of energy savings) yields results consistent with the findings in this chapter. See Benenson et al. (1978).

Table 22 Projected energy consumption in the United States in 2010, with energy savings[a,b]

Sector and end use	Total energy consumed in 1972 (quads)	Potential savings (percent)	Increased activity per capita in 2010[c] (percent)	Total energy consumption in 2010 (quads)	Footnote
Residential					
Space heating	7.1	67	112	3.1	3, 4, 5
Air conditioning	0.2	80	150	0.1	6, 7
Water heating	1.9	30	100	1.6	8, 9, 10
Appliances	0.7	40	120	0.6	11, 12
Other	0.8	40	120	0.7	11, 12
Subtotal[d]	10.6			6.1	
Electric generation losses	4.2			3.4	13
Total residential	14.8			9.5	
Transportation					
Automobile	9.1	75	120	3.7	14, 15
Air	2.2	50	300	4.4	16, 17
Truck	3.7	15	120	5.5	18, 19
Other	1.4	15	163	1.9	20, 21
Subtotal	16.4			15.5	
Electric generation losses	0			0.3	13
Total transportation[d]	16.5			15.8	
Commercial	5.9			7.8	
Electric generation losses	2.8			3.7	13
Total commercial	8.7	50	200	11.6	22, 23

Industrial

Energy consuming

Aluminum	0.6	47	118	0.5	24, 25
Agriculture	1.2	15	112	1.5	26
Cement	0.5	40	125	0.5	27
Chemicals (fuel and power)	3.1	26	163	5.0	28
Chemicals (feedstock)	1.6	0	163	3.5	29
Construction (asphalt)	0.9	42	132	0.9	30
Food	1.1	34	123	1.2	31
Glass	0.2	31	125	0.2	32
Iron and steel	3.1	28	118	3.6	33
Paper	2.2	43	132	2.2	34
Residual manufacturing and mining	5.6	43	132	5.7	35
Subtotal	20.1			24.8	
Electric generation losses	5.7			6.6	36

Energy producing

Methane production	2.0	0	55	1.5	37
Coal production	0.4	0	112	0.6	
Refinery use	2.5	40	75	1.5	38
Subtotal	4.9			3.6	
Electric generation losses	0.5			0.4	
Total industrial	31.2			35.4	
TOTAL	71.2			72.3	

[a]See footnote 1.
[b]All numbered footnotes appear in appendix to this chapter.
[c]See footnote 2.
[d]Totals may not add due to rounding.

Table 23 Summary of energy consumption scenario for the United States
in 2010

Factor	Year		Percentage of change
	1972	2010	
Population (millions)	207	278.8	+35
GNP (billion 1972 dollars)	1,500	2,862	+90
Energy consumption (quads)	71.2	72.3	+ 2
GNP, per capita (dollars)	7,246	10,264	+42
Energy consumption, per capita (million Btu)	343	259	−24

These energy-consumption figures refer to nonrenewable raw-energy
sources measured at the point of extraction (before cleaning, conversion, and transmission). In addition, the 2010 scenario includes about
4 quads of solar energy to provide some space heating and cooling and
hot-water heating. This amount of raw energy, measured at the point of
extraction, would otherwise have to be provided by nonrenewable resources
to maintain the comfort levels assumed. The solar-input equivalent was
calculated on the basis of the assumed savings factors for passive solar
houses and solar water heaters, on the per-capita energy consumption per
residential unit for the end uses affected (space heating and cooling
and water heating), and on the population, savings-factor, and activity-
level increases we postulated. We assumed that all other things were
held equal, but a number of factors could alter our calculation in either
direction. Among these are the extent of appliance saturation and the
fuels required, average house size, and the number of each type of residential unit. Thus the estimate of total energy use and the fossil-fuel
equivalent provided by solar energy is extremely tentative.

Although it is difficult to project total expenditures for energy
in 2010, it is assumed that the rise in energy prices is to some extent
offset by decreased per-capita energy consumption. Therefore, the proportion of personal consumption expenditures spent for energy goods and
services is assumed to remain near the historical percentage (approximately 10 percent) of the total GNP.

Much concern about decreased per-capita energy consumption is
focused on the relationship between energy and output, the assertion
being that if per-capita energy consumption were reduced, per-capita
production would decrease. However, the behavioral and technological

changes assumed in this scenario do not decrease the per-capita production of goods and services. Consumers retain approximately the same
levels of comfort in space heating and cooling and in water heating.
These services are merely delivered more efficiently, and some care is
taken in their use. Transportation services are used more efficiently.
For those who engaged in long commutes and experienced the accompanying
traffic jams of the 1970's, reductions in trips and vehicle miles traveled for conducting business and obtaining services may likely be perceived as a benefit rather than a hardship. Finally, in the industrial
and commercial sectors, the savings hypothesized per unit output do not
stem from production cutbacks but from more efficient energy use derived
from known technologies. However, the estimates in Table 23 of overall
energy consumption are affected by the GNP growth-rate assumption as
well as by the estimates of saturation and savings potential by sector.
For example, the assumed growth rate of overall industrial output, and
accordingly the growth rates of the particular industrial sectors as
delineated, enter the calculations directly as scaling factors of per-
capita energy consumption in industry. These assumptions are stated
explicitly in the footnotes to Table 22 (see the appendix to this chapter).

The above results relating income to energy use are in accord with
two conclusions of the Modeling Resource Group: that (1) GNP is an important determinant of the demand for energy, all else being equal, but
that (2) the reverse relationship may not hold because there appears to
be considerable opportunity for lowering the growth rate of energy with
only minor effects on real income.[a]

As long as the reduction of energy use is gradual and foreseen and
does not exceed the normal turnover of capital and labor, the reduction
could be absorbed without significant unemployment of capital and labor
(Nordhaus, 1976b; National Research Council, 1978). The analysis on
which these conclusions are based assumed that the government effectively
implements economic policy to maintain full employment.

Another important issue is the relationship between energy consumption and employment. This has been discussed in the more narrow context
of the employment impacts of energy conservation; it is argued that the
decision to cancel construction of a power plant (because of decreased
demand) means the loss of construction jobs. But this is too limited a

---

[a]This conclusion holds for an energy-price elasticity of -0.5 or greater.
As detailed by the CONAES Modeling Resource Group (National Research
Council, 1978), there is some econometric evidence to support the accuracy of this estimate (e.g., the work of Griffin and Gregory (1976) and
the empirical estimation of the demand curves in the Nordhaus model).
But the price-elasticity estimate is still in dispute. It is possible
that the elasticity is low enough so the cutbacks in energy use could
lead to significant cutbacks in real income. The energy growth rates
projected by the Modeling Resource Group indicate a long-run decline in
the ratio of energy use to GNP. Furthermore, the feedback through real
income to energy demand from all but the most drastic energy policies
is expected to be less than 2 percent of energy demand.

perimeter to draw around the issue of job impacts from energy conservation. The United States economy is extremely interrelated, with individual sectors buying from and selling to each other, thereby generating one another's income and employment. This interrelationship and the fact that energy-conservation measures usually require labor and materials lead to the conclusion that energy-conservation measures, while decreasing the demand for future energy production facilities, lead directly to expansion in other sectors.

For example, in the case of passive solar housing construction, expansion would occur in the glass and insulation industries and in the industries that produce materials for increasing shading and thermal mass. Additional employment would also be required at the construction site to install the materials that provide shading and thermal mass. At the same time, construction of power plants and attendant facilities would be dampened, resulting in employment cutbacks in these sectors. Thus income and employment changes in both directions are anticipated. The net impacts depend on the particular conservation measure in question and the type of power plant construction that is obviated.

MECHANISMS FOR IMPLEMENTING ENERGY CONSERVATION

The preceding material developed an energy scenario that embodies a significant amount of energy conservation. The results were given in detail in Table 22 and then summarized in Table 23. Footnotes to Table 22 described a number of energy-conserving measures and their associated energy savings. The question now arises about what might induce producers and consumers to adopt these measures. This section responds to this question by indicating some of the implementing mechanisms that could bring about substantial energy conservation. An attempt is made to anticipate some of the impacts and obstacles that might be associated with these mechanisms. This information is presented in a matrix of the implementing mechanisms (columns) and their potential impacts and obstacles (rows). The latter are used as a checklist. For a given implementing mechanism designed to reduce energy consumption, as assessment of the likely impact is made.

The results of this assessment are shown in Table 24. The number of impacts and obstacles presented is a subset of a larger list of potential impacts, some of which do not appear to apply to the particular conservation measures considered. Some other conservation measures, for example, may imply enforcement difficulties and changes in work rules; international economic impacts such as changes in the balance of payments; and locational impacts such as regional shifts in income and employment and tendencies toward demographic and economic centralization. (Impacts from policies in the transportation sector are included in the transportation chapter of the Demand and Conservation Panel (1976) draft.)

The matrix developed is intended to indicate problems and benefits associated with conservation measures. It is not a complete exposition of the impacts; nor is it an exhaustive list of the measures by which energy conservation may be induced. For example, retrofit installation

of storm windows and insulation could also be accomplished by encouraging utilities to adopt conservation loan programs. Energy-saving
features in multifamily houses could be obtained by building-code re-
visions. Increased installation of rooftop solar collectors for space
and water heat might be facilitated as much by educational programs
and building-code changes as by additional research and development.

Although the matrix is incomplete, several insights can be drawn
from developing it. First, there is a variety of policies and other
mechanisms by which energy-conservation measures could be implemented.
Second, both positive and negative impacts are likely to be associated
with their adoption; therefore it is advisable to anticipate as many
impacts as possible to mitigate the unintended consequences. Third, a
more general inferential conclusion is that there are likely to be both
positive and negative impacts from any energy policy, be it conservation-
oriented or production-oriented. Therefore, potential impacts and obstacles associated with the implementation of any energy policy should
be identified as clearly and completely as possible so that the alternatives can be meaningfully compared.

Table 24   Energy conservation policies and their impacts

Type of impact	Conservation measures and implementing policies								
	Retrofit insulation and storm windows (Economic incentive: homeowners' tax deductions for insulated storm windows)	Construction of multifamily houses (Economic incentive: loan guarantees for energy-saving features in multifamily housing construction)	Insulate water heaters; use 50 gallons per day at 120°F (Economic disincentive: meter hot water and tax at increasing rate above stipulated level)	Increase appliance efficiency (Economic disincentive: levy energy efficiency tax on appliances)	Construction of passive solar houses (Standards: specify passive solar housing characteristics in building code)	Increase appliance efficiency (Standards: establish appliance efficiency standards)	Lower thermostat; install thermostat clocks; heat part of house (Education: develop educational programs that explains monetary and energy savings from residential energy conservation measures)	General reduction of energy consumption (Market signals: energy price increases)	Install solar space and water heating equipment (Research/ Development: increase research and development toward lower cost solar collectors and water heaters)
Consumer									
Costs and benefits	Costs—time and money; benefits—energy and monetary savings	Decreased housing costs	Increased unit cost	Increased unit cost until producers are innovative; life-cycle cost decreases	Increased first cost of housing; decreased life-cycle cost	Increased first costs; decreased life-cycle costs	Decreased dollar expenditure for energy; costs incurred for energy-saving devices	Increased costs	–
Civil liberties	–	–	Water and energy use constrained	–	–	–	–	–	–
Equity	Benefits property owners more than renters unless landlord installs equipment for tenants	Favors middle, lower income groups	Regressive	Regressive	–	–	–	Greater impact on lower income groups	–
Public response	–	–	Probably negative	–	–	Positive from consumer interest groups	Potential negative response to suggestion of sacrifice	Negative	–
Industry									
Costs and benefits	–	Lower costs in construction industry	Costs to utilities to meter and bill customers	Costs increase to improve appliance efficiency	Increased costs to construction industry, passed on to consumer	May increase industry production costs; passed on to consumer	Costs to utilities if they undertake this program	Increased costs	May increase costs
Enforcement difficulties	–	–	Bill collection	–	–	–	–	–	May lead to union jurisdictional disputes for installation
Work rules	–	–	–	–	Construction temporarily disrupted	–	–	–	–

Response	—	—	—	Negative because first costs increased	Negative	Negative	—	Negative	—
Commerce Costs and benefits	—	Stimulates loan activity for bank	—	—	—	—	—	Increased costs	—
Response	—	—	—	Negative because first costs increased	—	Negative	—	Negative	—
Government Costs and benefits	Decreases revenue	Costs—guarantee fund and defaults	—	—	—	Inspection costs	Costs incurred if government sponsored	Increased costs	May incur cost
Enforcement difficulties	Spot inspections; labor costs	—	—	Tax may be confusing to calculate at point of sale	Same difficulties as enforcing present building codes	—	—	—	—
Legislative precedent	Tax deductions for interest on mortgage	Veterans loans	Lifeline rates for gas and electricity	Present excise taxes and graduated road tax on trucks	Present codes	Present appliance efficiency standards	—	—	—
Economic International	—	—	—	—	—	—	—	Unclear; may affect balance of payments favorably if energy imports decrease	Potentially favorable effect on balance of payments if exports increase
National: Income	Increase in glass, insulating sectors	Increase in housing, banking industries	Increase in revenue for utilities	—	Increase in sectors that produce materials for insulation, glazing, shading, and thermal mass	—	Increase to producers of energy-saving devices	Potential increase for energy suppliers	Increase for producers
Employment	Increase in glass, insulation sectors, also in installation services	Increase in housing, banking industries	Increased employment for meter production and installation	—	—	Potential increase in research	Increase to producers and installers of energy-saving devices	—	Increase in government or private industry
Political	—	—	Unpopular	—	—	—	—	Potentially strong	—
Locational	—	—	Regional movements of tax levels vary	—	—	—	—	—	May decentralize energy industry
Time frame to realize savings	1 to 5 years	Less than 5 years	Less than 5 years	Less than 5 years	5 to 10 years; linked to housing stock and rate of replacement	Less than 5 years	Uncertain	Uncertain	5 to 15 years after development

APPENDIX: NOTES TO TABLE 22

1. Sources: For residential, commercial, and transportation sectors,
    Beller (1975); for industrial sector, Richard W. Barnes, Dow Chemical
    U.S.A., from material developed for the Supply and Delivery Panel.

2. This factor may be interpreted as the percentage change in the per-
    capita consumption of the amenity for which energy is used. It is
    attributable to rising income for the following end uses: residen-
    tial space heating and cooling, and automobile and air transportation.
    For water heating, appliances, and other residential uses, the acti-
    vity estimates are based on a saturation factor unique to those
    appliances. The activity figures assigned to industry, commerce,
    and transportation are estimates of the per-capita growth rates of
    the sectors. We assume an overall increase of 0.8 percent per capita
    per year in industry, or a 32-percent increase over present produc-
    tion by 2010. Historically, some industries have exceeded the aver-
    age growth rate for the industrial sector as a whole and others have
    lagged behind it. The growth rates have therefore been adjusted to
    account for the potential continuation of this trend. Adjustment
    factors for each industry were computed by expressing historical
    growth rates of that industry as a percentage of the historical
    total industrial growth rate. These computations are shown in the
    table of annual growth rates (Table 25). The resulting assumed
    annual per-capita growth rates of these industries are as follows:
    aluminum, 0.48 percent; agriculture, 0.32 percent; cement, 0.64
    percent; chemicals (fuel and power), 1.4 percent; chemicals (feed-
    stock), 1.4 percent; construction (asphalt), 0.8 percent; food, 0.6
    percent; glass, 0.64 percent; iron and steel, 0.48 percent; paper,
    0.8 percent; residual manufacturing and mining, 0.8 percent. Over
    a 35-year period these growth rates yield the assumed increased
    activity per-capita figures shown in the third column of Table 22.

3. Lowering the thermostat from $72^{\circ}F$ during the day and to $55^{\circ}F$ at
    night results in a 37-percent saving. Applying ceiling and wall
    insulation, weatherstripping, and storm windows to half the houses
    yields a 25-percent saving. A 30-percent saving is obtained from
    heating only 70 percent of the house. Combining these measures
    results in a saving potential of 67 percent: $(1 - .37)(1 - .25)$
    $(1 - .30) = 0.33$, or 0.67 saving potential. Because the 67-percent
    saving factor is derived from retrofit measures, it applies to the
    old stock of houses still in use in 2010 (51.13 million units). The
    assumptions for all housing units are shown in Table 26. The poten-
    tial saving for new plus replacement units is estimated to be 72
    percent. The saving potential is applied to 53.87 million units
    (see Table 26). The 72-percent saving potential is derived by assum-
    ing a 65-percent saving from using 2" x 6" stud construction to per-
    mit more ceiling and wall insulation, a 10-percent saving from
    reduction of floor space by 10 percent, and a 10-percent saving from
    south-facing windows to increase heat gain and retention during the

Table 25 Annual growth rates by industry

Industry	Historical growth rate 1950–1973 (percent per year)	Growth rate adjustment factor
Total industry	4.38	1.0
Primary metals	2.45	0.6
Clay, glass, and stone products	3.42	0.8
Miscellaneous manufacturing	4.56	1.0
Paper	4.58	1.0
Chemicals	7.75	1.75
Food	3.18	0.75
Agriculture	1.74	0.4

Source: Bureau of the Census (1975b)

Table 26 Composition of residential units, in millions

Type	1976	2010			
		Old	Replacement[a]	New	Total
Single family	48.3	33.9	14.4	15.0	63.3
Multi-family	21.5	15.1	6.3	15.0	36.4
Mobile home	3.0	2.1	0.9	2.3	5.3
Total	72.8	51.1	21.6	32.3	105.0

[a]Assumes that existing stock dies off at 1 percent per year

Source: Adapted from Demand and Conservation Panel (1976)

winter. The calculations of total savings potential parallels the one given immediately above.

4. This factor implies that, as income rises, the expenditures for housing are made to obtain better location and quality and not to increase floor space greatly per capita (which would increase space-heating requirements). It is assumed that the number of people per housing unit decreases from the 1976 estimate of 2.94 to 2.37 for the additions plus replacements in 2010.

5. The 67-percent saving potential results in 0.01 quad of energy consumed per million people; the 72-percent saving potential for new plus replacement units results in energy consumption of 0.0096 quad per million people. The estimate of 3.06 quads of energy consumption in 2010 is a composite of both savings estimates applied to the appropriate housing stocks. The derivation is as follows:

51.13 (old housing stock in millions) x 2.94 (people per housing unit) = 150.32 million people residing in old houses to which retrofit measures apply.

150.32 x 0.0096 (quad per million people) x 112% (increased activity per capita) = 1.68 quads.

278 (population in millions, year 2010) - 150.32 (million people residing in old houses) = 128 (million people residing in new and replacement units to which new housing energy conservation measures apply).

128 x 0.0096 (quad per million people) x 112% = 1.38 quads + 1.68 = 3.06 quads.

6. The 80-percent saving potential is derived from the following conservation measures: increase thermostat setting by $2^{\circ}F$ (16-percent saving), open windows to cool when possible (20-percent saving), cool half the area of the house that is now cooled (50 percent), and install a high-efficiency window air conditioner (40 percent). The composite saving potential parallels the calculation in note 3 above.

7. A 50-percent per-capita increase in the units air conditioned is assumed.

8. The 30-percent saving potential is assumed to result from 4-5 inches of insulation installed, water use maintained at 50 gallons per day, and the temperature setting reduced to $120^{\circ}F$. The 30-percent saving is applied to the existing housing stock plus 40 percent of the new and replacement units (72.67 million units). A 65-percent saving potential is applied to the remaining new residential units (32.32 million). This assumes solar water heaters for 60 percent of the houses built after 1976, thermostat setting at $120^{\circ}F$, and water use maintained at 50 gallons per day.

9. Water heaters are assumed to saturate at the present per-capita consumption.

10. Energy consumption for conventional water heaters is calculated with a 30-percent saving potential as follows:

    1.87 quads/72.8 residential units in 1976 = 0.0256 quad per million units x 70 percent consumption = 0.0179 quad per million units x 72.67 (millions of existing plus 40 percent of new and replacement units) = 1.30 quads.

    For solar water heaters, an analogous calculation is made using 32.32 million residential units, to which is applied a 65-percent saving potential.

    Estimated energy consumption is 0.28 quad, to which is added 1.30 quads for conventional water heaters, yielding total estimated energy consumption of 1.58 quads.

11. A saving potential of 40 percent for all appliances and other residential end uses is assumed.

12. Appliances and other residential end uses are assumed to saturate at 1.2 times the present stock per capita.

13. This estimate is derived by multiplying total energy consumption for the residential sector by the assumed share for electricity and by the adjustment factor of 2.2349 (see Tables 27 and 28).

$$2.2349 = \frac{12.806 \text{ (energy dissipated in generating electricity by utilities, in quads)}}{5.730 \text{ (total electricity consumed, in quads)}}$$

Table 27 Electricity use as percentage of total energy per sector

Sector	Year	
	1972[a]	2010
Residential	17.6	25.0
Commercial	21.5	21.5
Industrial	11.9	14.8
Transportation	0.001	0.010

[a]Beller (1975)

Table 28 Electricity losses in quads per sector

Sector	Year	
	1972	2010
Residential	4.19	3.4
Commercial	2.83	3.7
Industrial	5.74	7.0
Transportation	0.04	0.3
Total	12.80	14.4

Source: Beller (1975)

14. The 75-percent saving estimate includes all measures described in Table 23 plus use of the 35-mpg car.

15. Automobiles are assumed to saturate at 1.2 times the present ownership per person.

16. The conservation measures that result in a 50-percent estimated saving are increasing the load factor from 0.5 to 0.7 (28 percent), increasing the average trip length and use of more-efficient ground transportation for shorter trips (14 percent), and increasing engine efficiency (10 percent).

17. Air travel per capita is assumed to increase by a factor of 3, which is a 4-percent annual per-capita increase in air passenger miles (see transportation chapter of Demand and Conservation Panel (1976)).

18. A 15-percent increase in efficiency is assumed (Source: transportation chapter of Demand and Conservation Panel (1976)).

19. The per-capita increase in trucking is assumed to scale at 0.5 percent per capita per year, which is less than the per-capita increase in industrial output. The slack is assumed to be taken up by an increase in rail transport and a reduction in empty backhauling.

20. A 15-percent efficiency increase is assumed.

21. It is assumed that rail scales more than the per-capita increase in industrial output because truck transportation is scaled down. The calculation is based on Table 3, "Freight Cargo Ton Miles per Year per Person by Function and Vehicle," from a preliminary draft of "Transportation Energy, Conservation and Demand Options to 2010," Demand and Conservation Panel (1976). All figures are expressed in freight cargo ton miles per year per person. The calculation is indicated below:

1972 total transportation (except oil pipeline) was 6626.95. Scaling up at 1 percent per year for 38 years gives 9672.21.

1972 total truck transportation was 2891.66. Scaling up at 0.5 percent per year gives 3495.08.

1972 certified domestic air transport was 16.29. Scaling up at 1 percent per year gives 23.77.

Subtracting 3495.08 and 23.77 from 9672.21 yields the residual left to rail: 6153.35 freight cargo ton miles per year per person.

Calculating the growth rate from the 1972 value of 3719 to 6153.35 for 38 years yields 1.013 per capita per year, or 1.63 overall.

22. Source: Buildings chapter of Demand and Conservation Panel (1976).

23. Per-capita commercial floor space is assumed to double.

24. For the industrial sector, the estimated savings and the material in the corresponding footnotes were provided by Richard W. Barnes from material developed for the CONAES Demand and Conservation Panel.

25. <u>Aluminum</u>

    (a) Recycle scrap generated during production. Approximately 19 percent of finished aluminum production represents scrap input that is recycled. Assuming high energy prices, approximately 50 percent of finished aluminum will be produced from recycled scrap, with 16 percent estimated saving.

    (b) Install new Alcoa process for aluminum smelting. Average energy consumption for smelting in 1972 was 7.7 kWh/lb. of aluminum. The new process requires 4.5 kWh/lb., for a saving factor of 42 percent. The breakdown of the major phases of aluminum production is given below:

Process	Btu/lb Aluminum
Refining	12,000
Smelting	26,000
Scrap reduction	6,000
Fabrication and holding furnaces	17,500
Total	62,000

Since smelting accounts for 42 percent of the energy consumed in aluminum production, overall saving attributable to this measure is approximately 18 percent.

(c) Basic housekeeping:

Plug leaks, reduce scrap, turn off unused lights, pumps, and motors, maintain optimum air to fuel ratio, use care in operating procedures (e.g., eliminate unnecessary reheating), have regular equipment maintenance.

(d) Waste-heat recovery:

(1) Redesign holding furnaces.
(2) Install Alcoa flash calcination process, which uses 30 percent less energy than present kilns.
(3) Preheat combustion air and cold aluminum with heat from melting furnaces, resulting in 61-percent improvement in thermal efficiency of furnace.

In general, the aluminum industry is expected to be responsive to energy-price increases because of the high energy content of aluminum. This response would work in favor of energy conservation, but two factors mitigate this tendency. First, the lower quality of raw materials expected to be available in the future will increase energy requirements. Second, the switch from gas to coal and oil with lower combustion efficiency will increase requirements. These factors are included in the estimates of energy savings.

26. Agriculture

In the agricultural sector there are trends working for and against energy conservation. Elements of both trends are listed below. The overall estimated saving of 15 percent is net.

Energy-conserving trends are:

(a) Conversion of farm machinery from gasoline to diesel is estimated to save 50 percent of the energy used for farm machinery The saving is approximately 0.1 quad, or 8 percent.

(b) Minimum tillage, 8 percent net. This results from a direct decrease in energy used for tilling, but more weed killers, which have a high energy content, are then required.

(c) Better machinery operation, 8 percent.

(d) Improved greenhouse operation.

(e) Improved crop drying.

(f) More efficient pumping for irrigation, probably offset by added irrigation requirements.

Energy-consuming trends are:

(g) Environmental controls reduce energy efficiency. They are not now a big factor, but they could become important if more stringent waste-disposal standards are adopted.

(h) More intensive land use for increased yield requires more fertilizer, herbicide, insecticides, and irrigation.

(i) If consumer preferences shift away from grain and toward meat, there may be as much as a 22-percent increase in energy requirements (0.26 quad).

(j) Increased agricultural exports.

27. <u>Cement</u>

(a) Switch from wet to dry process eliminates need to evaporate water from product.

(b) Waste heat is recovered by increasing the thermal mass of the kiln. This is accomplished by welding the ends of chains to the inside of the kiln; heat is quenched in the chains, which also help to grind the cement.

(c) Countering these saving measures is the shift from gas to coal, which requires energy to crush and grind it.

28. <u>Chemicals (Fuel and Power)</u>

(a) Housekeeping

(1) Maintain steam traps.
(2) Eliminate loss of steam and process heat.
(3) Reduce internal waste to reduce recycling.

(b)   Process change

    (1)   Use filtration instead of evaporation.
    (2)   Change catalysts, which changes yield but reduces energy consumption.

(c)   Waste-heat recovery

Several factors in the industry tend to increase energy consumption. Products that are most energy intensive are those that are growing the fastest (e.g., plastics, fertilizers, synthetic fibers, chemicals). If the historical trend continues, energy consumption in this sector will be high. The trend in the use of plastics in automobiles is illustrative: before 1975, 20 to 30 lb. of plastic was used in each automobile. In 1975, more than 100 lb. was used. By 1985-1990, 200-300 lb. is projected. The plastic is used as a substitute for steel to reduce weight and thus conserve fuel. If a net energy saving is achieved, this substitution has an obvious benefit. In the case of throwaway plastic containers and molded-plastic furniture, both of which are energy intensive and labor saving, many impacts are detrimental. From the point of view of energy and employment policy, the effects of differential growth rates in this industry should be explored.

29.   Chemicals (Feedstocks)

No savings are predicted. Products in this sector, such as naphtha, ethylene, and natural gas, are produced in petroleum refining. Their consumption is tied directly to the output of industries that use hydrocarbon feedstocks (e.g., plastics, synthetic fibers, fertilizers, and organic chemicals not elsewhere classified). Savings in the production of feedstocks are counted under refinery use (below).

30.   Construction (Asphalt)

(a)   Recycle old asphalt.

(b)   Substitute sulfur for asphalt.

31.   Food

(a)   Waste-heat recovery.

(b)   Housekeeping.

    (1)   Conserve hot water.
    (2)   Generate steam more efficiently.

The expenditure for energy represents a small percentage of the total dollar cost of food. No dramatic breakthroughs for energy savings have been foreseen. Since there has not been much incentive for energy conservation thus far, housekeeping practices are poor and substantial improvements can be made. (Potential savings were based on audits by Johns Manville.)

32. <u>Glass</u>

(a) Housekeeping.

(b) Waste-heat recovery.

(c) Recycling is limited because of consumer rejection of recycled glass. Not included in savings calculation.

(d) Deposits on bottles reduce growth projection.

Flat-glass production has undergone substantial modernization during the past several years, so the potential for additional improvement here is less than for the remaining segments of the industry.

33. <u>Iron and Steel</u>

Energy-conserving measures:

(a) Housekeeping.

(b) Process changes:

(1) Use form coking.
(2) Increase level of scrap available for recycling for an estimated 5 percent in energy saving.
(3) Use hot-metal charges in electric steel operation to reduce electric energy input by 15-20 percent.
(4) Use continuous casting to reduce reheating by consolidating operations within a plant and minimizing time spans between operations.

Energy-consuming trends:

(c) Environmental controls lead to an estimated 5-10-percent increase in energy input to produce equivalent product.

(d) Shift in customer preference to stainless and alloy (high-strength) steel may require twice as much energy as for production of carbon steel.

(e) Use of low-grade coal in form coking (see b, above) is more
energy intensive, although form coking still results in a net
energy saving.

34. <u>Paper</u>

Energy-conserving measures:

(a) Housekeeping has 5-15-percent energy-saving potential because
of present overall sloppiness in energy consumption.

(b) Recycle scrap generated internally.

(c) Waste-heat recovery.

Energy-consuming trends:

(d) Shift in consumer preferences toward more bleached paper.

(e) Use of scrap as fuel rather than as paper. A major debate
within the industry centers on whether to design a mill to
use internally generated paper scrap for paper or for fuel.
If scrap is used for paper, mechanical pulping is required
and purchased electricity increases, although overall energy
use is minimized. The alternative is to use scrap for energy,
which reduces purchased electricity requirements but increases
total energy requirements. In the maximum electricity-usage
case, it is assumed that one-third of the mills use mechanical
pulping and two-thirds use thermochemical pulping.

35. <u>Residual Manufacturing and Mining (Fabrication)</u>

(a) Housekeeping.

(b) Waste-heat recovery.

(c) Conversion to diesel engines.

There are large potential savings in these sectors because they
have not been very energy conscious to date.

36. It is assumed that electricity use scales with industrial output,
which is adjusted downward by 10 percent per unit of output for
assumed energy conservation induced by higher energy prices. The
calculation is shown below:

Elec-tricity use in industry (1972)	x	Industry growth rate per capita over 35 years	x	Percentage increase in population	x	Savings factor	=	Estimated electricity consumption in industry (2010)
2.6 quads	x	1.32%	x	135	x	0.10	=	4.1 quads

To estimate electricity-generation losses, it is assumed that one-third of electricity in 2010 is cogenerated. The losses are computed below:

	Electricity (quads)	Loss factor (percent)	Loss (quads)
Cogenerational	1.37	0.33	0.45
Conventional	2.77	2.2349	6.19
Total			6.64

For the derivation of the loss factor, see number 13, above.

37. For the energy-producing sectors, we assume that natural-gas production decreases by 25 percent (0.55 per capita), coal production increases by 50 percent (1.12 per capita), and oil production remains constant (0.75 per capita).

38. An efficiency increase of 40 percent in refinery use is assumed. This is consistent with the Btu/production unit calculations for scenario A of the Industry Resource Group's report to the Demand and Conservation Panel, in which real energy prices are assumed to quadruple. (The report is available in the CONAES public file.)

39. Losses are assumed to be approximately 10 percent of energy use.

REFERENCES

Austin, T. C., and K. H. Hellman. 1975. Passenger Car Fuel Economy as Influenced by Trip Length. Paper prepared for national meeting of the Society of Automotive Engineers, Feb. 1975, Detroit.

Beller, M., ed. 1975. Source Book for Energy Assessment. Upton, N.Y.: Brookhaven National Laboratory. December.

Benenson, P., R. Cordina, B. Cornwall, D. Dornfeld, B. Greene, J. Elliott, W. Kempton, C. Langlois, H. Nelson, J. Nides, F. Rouse, and C. Sullam. 1978. Energy Conservation: Policy Issues and End-Use Scenarios of Savings Potential. Berkeley, Calif.: Lawrence Berkeley Laboratory (LBL 7896).

Bureau of the Census. 1975a. Historical Statistics of the United States, Colonial Times to 1970. Chapter G. Consumer Expenditure Patterns. Washington, D.C.: U.S. Department of Commerce.

Bureau of the Census. 1975b. Statistical Abstracts of the United States. Washington, D.C.: Social and Economic Statistics Administration, U.S. Department of Commerce.

Bureau of Economic Analysis. 1976. Survey of Current Business 56(1), Parts 1 and 2. Washington, D.C.: U.S. Department of Commerce.

Demand and Conservation Panel. 1976. Draft report to the Committee on Nuclear and Alternative Energy Systems, National Research Council, Washington, D.C.: National Academy of Sciences.

Griffin, J. M., and P. R. Gregory. 1976. An Intercountry Translog Model of Energy Substitution Responses. American Economic Review, December.

Hise, E. C., and A. S. Holman. 1975. Heat Balance and Efficiency Measurements of Central, Forced Air, Residential Gas Furnaces. Oak Ridge, Tenn.: Oak Ridge National Laboratory (ORNL-NSF-EP-88). October.

Kravis, I. B., Z. Kenessey, A. Heston, and R. Summers. 1975. A System of International Comparisons of Gross Product and Purchasing Power. Baltimore: Johns Hopkins University Press.

Moyers, J. C. 1971. The Value of Thermal Insulation in Residential Construction: Economics and the Conservation of Energy. Oak Ridge, Tenn.: Oak Ridge National Laboratory (ORNL-NSF-EP-9). December.

National Research Council. 1978. Energy Modeling for an Uncertain
Future. Modeling Resource Group, Synthesis Panel, Committee on
Nuclear and Alternative Energy Systems. Washington, D.C.: National
Academy of Sciences.

National Research Council. 1979. Alternative Energy Demand Futures to
2010. Demand and Conservation Panel, Committee on Nuclear and Alternative Energy Systems. Washington, D.C.: National Academy of Sciences.

Nordhaus, W. D. 1976a. Compiled in CONAES memo, June 7, 1976.

Nordhaus, W. D. 1976b. What Is the Tradeoff Between Energy Consumption
and Real Income? Paper prepared for CONAES, October 27, 1976.

Pilati, D. A. 1976. Residential Energy Savings Through Modified
Control of Space-Conditioning Equipment. Energy 1:233–239.

Quinn, R. S., Jr. 1972. The Effect of Increased Capital Expenditures
as a Method of Reducing Electricity Demand for Hot Water Generation
in New Homes. M.Sc. Thesis, University of Tennessee, Knoxville.
August.

U.S. Federal Highway Administration. 1969. Nationwide Personal
Transportation Survey. Prepared for U.S. Department of
Transportation. Washington, D.C.: U.S. Government Printing Office.

6 NEW ATTITUDES TOWARD ENERGY AND RESOURCES:

A HIGH-TECHNOLOGY, LOW-ENERGY SOCIETY

The scenario[a] described in this chapter is an exercise based on a world
in which a relatively high standard of living is compatible with an
approximate 50-percent per-capita reduction in energy consumption--an
apparently contradictory situation. It is not intended to predict the
future[b]; rather it explores the questions: What could life be like in
the United States if, instead of increasing energy use per capita, or
keeping it constant, we reduced it substantially? Would the consequences of a 53-quad society be as horrible as some imagine? Would they be
as beneficial as others claim?

---

[a]The realization that a 72-quad society required minimum behavioral
change led us to explore what the dominant living patterns might be in
a 53-quad scenario. We were further encouraged to explore the concept
of a society of low energy expenditure and high efficiency since it
appeared that much of the work of the CONAES study would be at the
other end of the continuum.

[b]To an extent that would appall scientists in disciplines accustomed to
relatively closed systems, behavioral interactions consist of a vast
network in which virtually everything is dynamically related to everything else. In the present case, location decisions, transportation
modes, and consumption of other goods and services are all interrelated.
As a result, changes in behavior with respect to one activity often
affect other activities. For example, restrictions on energy use for
heating home swimming pools might shift leisure activity away from homes
and onto the highways. It was clear as we worked through our task that
our resource group's function was necessarily multidimensional; it had
to be a synthesis.

This chapter presupposes a fairly substantial shift in the values that guide individual choice in the marketplace. It assumes that by the year 2010 some values that were once prominent in the hierchy of values have taken on renewed importance. These values are self-reliance, thrift, individual freedom, and, perhaps paradoxically, attachment to one's community. Such a resurgence of old-fashioned virtues is seen not as an expression of nostalgia for a world we have lost but as an adaptation to the post-World War II world and an extrapolation into the future of present apprehensions about resources. This scenario emphasizes survival.

These underlying shifts in attitudes toward energy and resources are motivated by an awareness that the affluence enjoyed by some in the United States is in striking contrast to poverty here and in most of the world and by the realization that resources are finite. Change may stem from the reflection that present patterns, including high energy use, have brought even the recipients less rather than more well being and that per-capita GNP has not been a useful measure of the welfare of a population--as disclosed, for example, by various assessments of the quality of life. A more pragmatic reason to think about change is that it may be forced on us. Even if we genuinely prefer a society consuming 72 quads or more per year by 2010, we may not be able to get it.

We found that the scenario technique was useful as an exercise in which to explore interrelations while keeping certain assumptions constant. The prose is an attempt to illustrate kinds of behavior that are compatible with one another. The synthetic information in the prose scenario constructions could have been stated as postulates, for example: High unemployment is found in increasing association with rising crime rates; an active consumer movement is incompatible with high unemployment; an increase in self-employment is compatible with increasing self-reliance, increasing individual productivity, and increasing worker satisfaction; growing one's own food may be associated with a decrease in food waste; energy systems that are highly vulnerable to sabotage are compatible with a more active police force and a less democratic form of government.

As for its utility for policy makers, the scenario technique can be misleading unless the policy makers understand the limitations of the technique. This may be true also of economic models. There is not just one way to get to an energy level of 70 or 100 quads, but many ways. Furthermore, we may ignore the observation that our vision of the future affects the present; the future then becomes in part a self-fulfilling prophecy. Scenarios are not objective. A scenario may be bound by premises that we do not recognize. It may tacitly reflect the premise of industry, or it may reflect the premises underlying various analytical models. It may tacitly reflect the distribution of power in society today. It is important in this work to attend to the range of self-interest of both writers and audiences to ease the problems posited by the notion of equitable planning.

In this scenario, a large proportion of the public has lost its commitment to economic growth. America's losing battle for high-growth energy independence, public perplexity over the risks of nuclear power and the world-wide proliferation of nuclear weapons capabilities, greater environmental change resulting from economic growth and energy use, and increased awareness of our energy position relative to the rest of the world--in spite of increasing optimism concerning the harnessing of solar energy--are only some of the factors that might lead to altered values. It is as if people had begun to believe that, although it is nice for any individual to become rich, the problems created by everyone's becoming rich began to outweigh the benefits of the higher income. Thus the scenario assumes that average per-capita income as currently measured will stop growing and remain at about 1977 levels; the lot of the poor will be improved substantially through redistribution of income and wealth.

A world with no economic growth as we know it may strike many readers as incredible. No doubt it requires altering our assumptions about individual and social aspirations. If present poor families are to have an opportunity to improve their position, other families must limit their use of energy and resources. In short, it is not absurd to suppose that sufficiently many Americans may come to regard less as more. There can be many opportunities for individual mobility--up or down--even in a no-growth society. In fact, there is fragmentary evidence of voluntary downward mobility among many college and professionally educated young people of the 1970's. If our data on career histories were as good as those on income, we would know better whether this is a significant trend or not.[a]

Whether or not such a general value change will appear among the generation running the United States in 2010, and in their children and grandchildren, we cannot say. Many people believe that it will. Therefore, we should seriously try to imagine what the consequences of such changes might be.

Life in 2010 would appear externally similar to life in the 1970's. We see buses and trains throughout the country, although in larger numbers than in earlier years. Fewer cars are on the highways, and these are smaller, lighter, and more efficient than the cars of the 1970's.

There are still large cities, although the urban congestion of previous years has been greatly reduced. In all the large urban centers, city shopping, business, and cultural activities continue to flourish, but as one moves into areas surrounding the core city, one finds centers for industrial arts, social life, and services in use every day of the week. The tone of activity is changed; people move at a more leisurely pace and seem to be dressed for comfort.

----

[a]See, for example, Wall Street Journal (1976), Berton (1969), Linder (1970), and Callenbach (1972) for discussions of why downward mobility might be attractive to some.

DRIVING FORCES AND ADAPTIVE STRATEGIES

As new economic and social concerns became national priorities in the
1970's, people developed a multitude of adaptive strategies varying from
simple conservation to more complicated measures: changes in residence,
occupation, home construction, automobiles, appliances, and modes of
public transportation. These strategies developed out of people's conscious efforts to deal effectively with energy and resource scarcity,
increased prices, and the fact that energy forms have environmental and
social risks attached to them in varying degrees.

Congestion in cities and suburbs was becoming increasingly stressful in the late 1970's, and without more efficient cars and public
transportation for short trips, the quality of life in the deteriorating
environment was dropping sharply. With real shortages in nonrenewable
energy resources foreseeable in the near future, people began to realize
that certain needs could no longer be met by more of the same technology.
Increasing attention was paid to responsible uses of space, time, intel-
lect, and resources. Movement out of the cities had produced stressful
situations for millions of people who found they were spending hard-
earned nonworking hours fighting traffic, noise, exhaust, congestion,
tension headaches, and other symptoms of the inverse relation between
increasing income and satisfaction.

By 2010, time-saving technology and a shorter work week have created more leisure--or more independent time for creative projects.
People have filled their free time with sports (fishing, hiking, cycling),
reading, CB radios, art, cinema, music, and recreational and social
activities. Art centers, cultural centers, and libraries have blos-
somed. More crucial perhaps has been the reevaluation of the meaning
of time: it is now something to be used rather than invested. The
need for private automobiles has been reduced by fleets of small service
trucks performing errands and deliveries for companies and individuals.
Industrial service and commercial buildings show some clustering, although not all aspects of business have been decentralized. Because
workers want to live close to their places of work and still be close
to essential services and commercial areas, the tendency has been for
decentralization wherever possible. Services such as the telephone
remain primarily centralized, although repair, maintenance, and installation stations are more numerous and serve more localized communities.

A modified view of the relation between energy and work was developed with some struggle and difficulty in the 1980's. All labor is now
counted as work and is valued as part of the GNP. A major effect of no
growth has been an increase in self-employment, stimulated by government aid to small businesses, particularly to encourage work in areas
related to primary human needs. The increased numbers of self-employed
people demonstrate the desire to make work schedules more flexible.
Although in the 1970's some unions were a barrier to organizational
change, by 2010 unions are less concerned with wage increases and more
concerned with structuring jobs to make them more personally rewarding
and less depersonalizing.

ADVANCED TECHNOLOGY AND TASTE CHANGES

In 2010, as in the 1960's and 1970's, popular consumption of high-technology items still exists. High-fidelity phonograph systems are one familiar example, but advances in micro-solid-state devices have made small calculators, computerized games for television screens, and even home video-tape equipment within the reach of those in the medium as well as high income brackets.

The most important inputs to these devices are not energy or materials but knowledge and information, two factors that decline in relative cost as technology advances. The net effect of the increased use of these devices is to lower the energy impact of an average dollar of personal consumption, because the devices are not energy intensive. Advanced telecommunications equipment permits video communication to replace a sizable part of travel to work and intercity travel, especially when the purpose of the travel is to move data and information rather than to further personal contact. Bell Telephone Company information operators who prefer to work at home, for example, can do so.

The rapid advances in solid-state technology, however, have an even more direct impact on energy use. Small integrated systems can be designed to control energy use in climate conditioning, injection of fuel and air into automobile engines, the balancing of air and fuel in industrial boilers, and the optimization of electrified industrial processes involving many types of motors, conveyor belts, and lifts. Computers decide where to put the heat or electricity, and when. Even in the early 1970's some companies offered on-line computer systems that would monitor and control the energy used in large buildings, and it was anticipated that by 2010 minicomputers would be controlling the heating and cooling of properly insulated rooms in new homes more efficiently than could a single thermostat for an entire dwelling.

By 2010 we use information to reduce the need for materials, transportation, labor, and, more importantly, energy. We model energy use for buildings on high-speed computers, and we design systems that closely match true energy needs in the buildings themselves, rather than overdesigning systems to back up our ignorance of those needs. We use computer-coded structural analysis to pare down the material cost of building, which also reduces energy needs. We equip small trucks, mini-buses, and taxis with two-way radios that allow them to minimize the distances traveled; we use computers to control airplane movements, avoiding much of the formerly energy-wasteful circling of stacks of planes waiting for clearance over a single airport. In these and many other ways we find that technology plays an important role in maximizing the benefits we obtain from using energy and other resources.

Large buildings and houses look different from the way they used to look, though many factors in their construction and operation have not changed. The heat-admitting clear glass of solar passive heating does make buildings look different from the outside. Within limits, people in offices now have the luxury of controlling their own room temperature. Rooms and offices are pleasantly cool, but not as cold as supermarkets used to be. A number of industrial and commercial buildings of the last

30 years have been constructed underground, increasing the energy efficiency of these buildings and at the same time leaving more open space
in the communities.

Approximately 50 percent of the population lives in single-family
houses, but many owners have reduced costs in their heating and cooling
systems by sharing single units between two houses. The fraction of
duplexes has increased, as has that of trailers. Most houses and buildings have solar water-heating units which resemble the old evaporative
coolers of the Southwest on the roofs. In some areas, such as the
Pacific Northwest, Midwest, and Northeast, these solar units are supplemented by electric heat pumps or wind power during certain periods of
the year.

Travel from Seattle to San Francisco and Los Angeles, Denver to
Laramie, Boston to Washington, Dallas to Atlanta, and similar distances
is available on trains that are fast, silent, clean, and comfortable.
These trains deposit passengers at several different stations within an
urban area or at a single central location where buses, vans, taxis, and
small rental cars are available for trips to the final destinations. In
addition, car-trains transport people and vehicles over heavily traveled
long distances.

Trains and buses are also used heavily by people going to work and
to recreation areas, parks, concerts, restaurants, and sporting events;
for shopping, visiting friends, or just seeing the city. Most adults own
a small- or medium-sized fuel-efficient (30-35 mpg) automobile, though
some, depending on the neighborhood and lifestyle, own only a bicycle or
light motor scooter. Some individuals and families prefer to share
ownership of an automobile, which they use for longer vacation trips,
visits to relatives in other areas, and special shopping expeditions.
Multiple ownership of cars permits people to get away on trips but
divides the operation and maintenance costs of the cars, which are sel-
dom needed for local transportation.

The idea of ethnic or interest-group neighborhoods has spread more
widely throughout the nation than it had in 1975, and groups have clustered in various dispersed ways. Although some stores in each neighborhood try to stock a variety of food items, many people find it more
interesting and pleasant to frequent the neighborhoods for special food
items, or to travel to nearby experimental farms. Such excursions are
viewed as recreation for adults and education for children.

Experimental farming and industrial communities are dotted throughout the countryside in most areas of the country. Population in these
communities ranges from 5,000 to 30,000, depending on what energy forms
are used. In many of these communities local industry produces the
necessary electricity by cogeneration. Many households are engaged in
agriculture and cottage industry, which are part of a series of experiments with different energy, waste, industrial, and technical systems.
These systems are developed out of national and local research and development programs are then put to practical experiment in various parts of
the country. Some are regionally specific, whereas others have more
widespread applicability. The success of this type of community has
meant that the sifting and turnover time from inception to practical

application of new ideas has been greatly reduced; this has also led to
a proliferation of regional arts and crafts and technological and industrial inventions.

A SHIFT IN VALUES

The people of America in 2010 are thrifty. They have become sensitive
to world food needs. The world competition for food has also increased
the cost of grain and animal protein to the point at which waste is no
longer tolerated and is certainly not a way of displaying status. There
are fewer disposable items; people have come to value an item or product
and keep it for a longer period of time, avoiding the costs in time,
money, and movement of constant replacement. This attitude has generated
over the years a growth in the service and natural-products areas--more
cotton, linen, wood, stone, and natural-fiber construction. Synthetics
are still used when clearly superior to less energy-intensive materials.

The propensity to consume more and to waste an ever-growing percentage of what was produced was gradually seen as characteristic of a
devaluation of natural and human production and of future generations.
Early in American history, Benjamin Franklin had cautioned that a penny
saved is a penny earned and that haste, instead of being an end in
itself, makes waste. Gradually, through 200 years of growth, expansion,
war, and prosperity, the cautionary voice of thrift and savings had been
muffled and the sharp distinction between acquisition and acquisitive-
ness blunted.

Equating public welfare for some, and comfort and status for others,
with quantified productivity is one way of organizing a nation. But
Americans gradually learned that growth in the GNP did not necessarily
lead to the good life for the nation or for the individual. By the mid-
1970's, the concept of the GNP as a measure of the good life was already
being challenged by thoughtful economists. Although the GNP continued
to rise, homicide rates rose as well, with a greater incidence of anony-
mous homicide than before World War II.

Violent crime was on the increase, and this violence was being
perpetrated by people of a younger average age than in previous periods.
The suicide rate had remained relatively constant since 1900, but the
rate among younger people was higher. Americans were spending less
money on children's welfare (child care, medical care, education, and
services) than were the other major industrialized nations. Their infant
mortality rate was higher and their life expectancy lower than in many
industrialized countries. Americans were also enjoying less vacation
time and ate smaller amounts of fresh fruits and vegetables than did
people in Western Europe. (See Tables 29-31.)

Basic things--the postal service, new cars, medical-care systems,
insurance, or household appliances--seemed not to work well any more.
Complaint studies revealed that Americans voiced complaints about 25
percent of all goods and services they were purchasing (Best and
Andreasen, 1977). It was becoming harder and harder to introduce simple,
sensible changes (even if based on local consensus) in bureaucracies:

Table 29   International comparisons of vacation times in 1967

Country	Percentage of adult population taking vacations of six days or more
Sweden	66
Great Britain	64
Switzerland	62
Netherlands	59
Denmark	54
Norway	51
France	49
Luxembourg	47
Austria	41
West Germany	38
Belgium	37
Ireland (Republic)	36
Finland	35
Spain	32
Italy	28
Portugal	27
Weighted average of above countries	44
United States	27.7[a]

[a]Estimate based on census data

Source: Scitovsky (1976). Reprinted from The Joyless Economy: An Inquiry into Human Satisfaction and Consumer Dissatisfaction by Tibor Scitovsky. Copyright 1976 by Oxford University Press, Inc. Reprinted by permission.

Table 30 Quality of food: High-quality variants as a proportion of
total consumed

Country	Fruit (percent fresh)	Vegetables (percent fresh or frozen)	Butter and margarine (percent butter)	Meat (percent fresh or frozen[a])
Italy	97.9	76.7	99.9	93.9
France	93.3	79.4	84.7	94.7
Belgium	89.6	80.8	51.9	86.6
Sweden[b]	87.3	82.5	46.2	76.3
German Federal Republic	87.2	81.6	46.0	92.7
Netherlands	80.9	72.2	10.8	84.6
United Kingdom	72.8	72.5	67.8	90.4[c]
Weighted average for above countries	87.2	77.6	68.6	90.5
United States	62.0	67.4	34.0	66.0

[a]Excluded from this category are ground meat, fresh sausage, and
sausage meat.

[b]Swedish percentages are in terms of value.

[c]Probably an overestimate; includes ground meat, for which exact data
are unavailable.

Source: Scitovsky (1976). Reprinted from The Joyless Economy: An
Inquiry into Human Satisfaction and Consumer Dissatisfaction by Tibor
Scitovsky. Copyright 1976 by Oxford University Press, Inc. Reprinted
by permission.

Table 31 Life expectancy and infant mortality in developed countries[a]

Country	Life expectancy at birth			Infant mortality per 1000 births
	Total	Male	Female	
Sweden	74.1	71.7	76.5	11.1
Netherlands	73.9	71.0	76.7	12.1
Norway	73.5	71.0	76.0	12.8
Iceland	73.5	70.8	76.2	13.2
Denmark	73.3	70.8	75.7	14.2
France	72.4	68.6	76.1	17.1
Switzerland	72.1	69.2	75.0	14.4
Canada	72.0	68.8	75.2	17.6
United Kingdom	72.0	68.8	75.1	17.5
United States (white only)	71.9	68.3	75.7	16.8
United States (total)	71.1	67.4	74.9	19.2
German Democratic Republic	71.8	69.2	75.0	18.0
Israel	71.8	70.1	73.4	19.7
Bulgaria	70.8	68.8	72.7	24.9
Ireland (Republic)	70.8	68.6	72.9	19.6
Italy	70.7	67.9	73.4	28.3
Japan	70.6	69.1	74.3	12.4
Belgium	70.6	67.7	73.6	19.9
German Federal Republic	70.6	67.6	73.6	23.3

[a]1971 estimate or latest available

Source: Scitovsky (1976). Reprinted from <u>The Joyless Economy: An Inquiry into Human Satisfaction and Consumer Dissatisfaction</u> by Tibor Scitovsky. Copyright 1976 by Oxford University Press, Inc. Reprinted by Permission.

Social Security, welfare, universities, scientific laboratories, or
credit card companies. Business, industrial managers, and technicians
were admitting that they had real and sometimes insoluble operating problems. All in all, citizens were feeling increasingly that more money
was not equivalent to better living.

People began to question the general mechanism by which planners and
administrators preferred to deal with symptoms rather than underlying
causes. Citizens were concerned that some forms and systems of energy
production might be too vulnerable to human and organizational error,
or subject to sabotage and theft, and might put us into a system of
spiraling costs and diminishing returns. People began to demand serious
consideration of energy sources that were relatively inexhaustible, not
dangerous to human life or the larger environment, easy to locate in
clustered cities, communities, or individual buildings, and with fewer
social and economic costs for succeeding generations. Solar energy has
thus become the favored energy source of the twenty-first century.

As the world gradually became a smaller place through swifter travel, the utilization of land area, rainfall, and sunshine per capita began
to be essential factors in American reassessment of cooperation and competition at all levels: at home, at work, during recreation, in the
region, in the country as a whole, and within the world community. As
Americans became aware of their primary problems and organized to plan
effectively, they began to be aware of solutions to similar problems in
other nations. It was found that in Europe, where people had been
crowded in cities, plagued with pollution, and beset with high energy
prices years before the United States, certain countries had developed
interesting economies of space and energy.

In Sweden, with roughly the same per-capita income as the United
States, only 55-65 percent as much energy was used per capita as in the
United States (Schipper and Lichtenberg, 1976). Swedes were able to
extract higher efficiency in the large areas of transportation, materials
processing and space heating. This was primarily because in the 1970's
Swedish energy prices were high relative to those in the United States,
but also because of different attitudes about conservation and waste that
led to less ostentation in energy-consuming areas. The American second
car was replaced in Sweden by efficient, extensive mass transit. Swedish
cars were lighter (average weight 1100 kg versus 1700 kg in the United
States), partly because the distances usually traveled were smaller than
those in the United States.

West Germany, too, was shown in the 1970's to be more effective in
energy planning and use in a number of ways (Stanford Research Institute,
1975). Like the United States, Germany was dominated by automobile
travel, but it also had a higher proportion of more energy-efficient
buses, streetcars, and train cars per capita. Americans continued to
move city freight by truck and by pipelines; Germans used rails. Americans had larger dwelling units with a greater percentage of space heated
than did the Germans, who heated 45 percent of their living space. The
Germans had a larger ratio of apartments to single-family dwellings and
did not heat their bedrooms; this is still common practice in most of
Europe. The German per-capita energy use for cooking was 60 percent less

than that in the United States, where members of many families did not
eat meals together. In the commercial and industrial sector, 28 percent
of the electricity in Germany was efficiently generated by self-producers
rather than by large utilities; only 5 percent was self-generated in the
United States at the time.

Comfortable living patterns were possible within the limits of efficiency, conservation, and planning. In the wake of rising prices,
resource scarcity, a growing sense of self-reliance, and clustered communities, people began to demand sensible and creative solutions.

Some of the changes necessary to get from 1975 to 2010 were relatively simple and of a technical nature; the more difficult were intellectual and moral and penetrated all social and economic segments of our
society, mainly through informal means. Some changes were set by statute
and enforced: building codes, tax and loan incentives for conservation,
pollution standards, and utility rate structures (such as penalty rates
for peak load periods). But the vast majority of energy improvements in
the 53-quad society of 2010 were due to the will and concern of the population and the leadership they chose to represent them. The results are
summarized in Table 32.

Private/Residential

By 2010, several compelling factors have led individuals and families to
cluster in multi-unit housing of the duplex, apartment, or modular type:
high property taxes, higher energy prices, the isolation and anonymity
of urban apartment living, a decreased demand in some segments of the
population for privacy to the point of isolation, increased belief that
an intergenerational mix is desirable in living areas, and the increased
attraction of the idea of support groups--sharing household and child-
care responsibilities with people of similar tastes and habits. Repair,
craft, and service shops are everywhere, as are branch libraries. All
these factors fit into a more general picture of gradually decentralized
work, service, and living groups. Population density is relatively low
in nonurban areas, and clustered settlement patterns have left wide
expanses of land open for use.

Various social trends apparent by the 1970's have continued: emi-
gration from cities to the suburbs, movement from suburbs to rural or
suburban countryside, proliferation of communal farms, efforts to revi-
talize urban centers for convenient and pleasant living, cottage-industry
communities, and, unfortunately, a growing use of alcohol and other
drugs. A renewed sense of pioneerism and self-reliance inspired people
to begin growing their own produce, to keep small livestock, to switch
to natural grains, and to substitute vegetable and grain protein for
large quantities of meat; but these practical changes themselves have
caused dislocation not unlike the earlier shift of population from rural
to urban. In particular, employment shifts, social security programs,
the changing expectations of women, and the alienation of the elderly
are of grave concern.

Table 32 Energy use in the attitudes-changed scenario

Units	Energy consumed in 1972 (quads)	Potential savings (percent)	Activity per capita relative to 1972	Energy consumed in 2010 (quads)	Footnote number
Residential					
Space heating	7.13		1.0		
Existing stock		67	1.0	1.62	1
New stock		72	1.0	1.03	2
Air conditioning	0.21	70	(1.5)	0.09	3
Water heating	1.87				
Existing stock		30	1.0	1.26	4
New stock		65	1.0	0.24	5
Appliances	0.66	40	1.0	0.53	6
Other	0.75	25	1.0	0.59	7
Subtotal	10.63			5.36	
Electricity generation losses	4.19	76		3.32	2,12
Total	14.82			8.98	

Transportation					
Autos	9.12	0.70	0.77	2.84	8
Air	2.2	0.50	1.5	2.2	9
Trucks	3.66	0.15	1.0	4.18	10
Other	1.45	0.15	1.2	2.06	11
Subtotal	16.44			11.28	
Electricity generation losses	0.04			0.25	12
Total	16.48			11.53	
Commercial	5.88	0.45	1.1	3.90	13
Electricity generation losses	2.82			1.91	12
Total	8.70			5.81	
Industrial	25.00	0.30	0.9	20.95	14
Electricity generation losses	6.20			6.30	12,15
Total	31.20			27.25	
Grand total[b]	71.20			53.57	

[a] All numbered footnotes appear in the appendix to this chapter.

[b] Details may not add due to rounding.

These growing trends, combined with a general education and advertising campaign geared to help people respond effectively to increasing energy prices, led to some fundamental changes in consumption, work, and leisure among different segments of the population, which added up to a more differentiated society and to population shifts.

The regional distribution of populations has historically shifted to follow the location of business and industry (i.e., jobs). High-density metropolitan areas continued to grow until 1970, but the trend from 1970 to 1975 indicated a movement out of the metropolitan areas. The densely urban Northeast and the industrial centers of the North-Central region lost population while the West and South gained. Additionally, the movement from metropolitan urban areas to lower density areas continued. However, the technologies of the 1970's that made suburban life seem to have some of the advantages of rural life could not sustain that advantage later because of offsetting disadvantages such as cost in commuting time. In 2010, the counterurbanization movement is reflected in a different pattern: in clusters of small communities away from major urban centers but near sources of employment and services.

The differences and divergences can be overstated; some people still use private automobiles as well as energy-intensive appliances and products frequently, but nearly everyone has made some degree of trade-off between high energy prices and the self-defined necessities of the good life.

We have seen population increase from 214 million in 1975 to 280 million in 2010 and the number of households has increased from 72 million to 109 million. With intensive solar research and development incentives in the 1980's, residential demand for fuel and for electricity in general was reduced from the projected figures of 38 quads to 8.7 quads.[a] A conservative estimate suggests that solar water heating will make the greatest impact; solar space heating will be next in importance, with air conditioning a distant third.

Some of the saving in energy use for buildings comes from changing appliance use habits, but larger savings come from greater thermal integrity of structures, the greater technical efficiency of appliances, the increase in the proportion of multiple-family dwellings, and the direct use of solar energy (Pilati, 1976).

One way in which the heating needs of communities are met economically is through district heating, in which heat is carried from a small (80-100-MW-thermal) heating plant directly to apartments or houses. Fuel can be burned at a high temperature to generate steam to produce electricity. The "waste" heat can then be used to supply the district heating system with warm water, the temperature of which can be easily matched to the needs of homes and buildings. Excess electricity is channelled into a regional network when local demand is low and drawn from that same net when local demand exceeds local supply. The technical advantage of this combined system is that one unit of fuel can produce roughly 0.25 units of electricity and 0.5 units of heat; had the two

---

[a]Extrapolation from Table 22, in the high-energy scenario.

products been generated separately, in power stations and individual boilers, they would have required about 1.4 units of fuel.

These district heating systems demonstrate that there is a middle ground between highly centralized systems in which heat might be prepared in a single system for hundreds of thousands of homes, and highly decentralized systems in which each dwelling unit has an independent heating unit.

What was initially attractive about these systems was the possibility that they could be scaled to fit apartment/service complexes, which were being built as early as the 1970's. The most important factor in measuring the feasibility of such a system, beyond the saving in energy costs themselves, was the density of structures and population in the immediate area. As families and businesses began to move toward concentrated living and working communities, the necessary density was easy to achieve. Advances in pollution control made the district station adaptable to nearly any kind of burnable fuel, which made it possible to serve regions such as the Northeast and Midwest with solar-generated hydrogen from the Southwest and ocean sites (Bockris, 1975), supplemented by locally converted garbage, agricultural products, and fossil fuels.

One system available for study in the 1970's was the Swedish city of Malmo, where 915 MW of energy from electric generating plants were combined with a district heating system (Schipper and Lichtenberg, 1976). Of the primary input energy, only 26 percent was wasted, with 53 percent going to heat and 21 percent to electricity. Combined-cycle systems, such as gas turbines heated by the exhaust of fluidized bed combustors, offered the possibility of high efficiency for electricity generation combined with low pollution levels. The Dow Chemical Company (1975) estimated that cogeneration, using combined-cycle and diesel systems, could produce 90 percent of New Jersey's energy by 1985.

In the early years of planning for major electricity, steam, and heating needs during energy scarcity, planners sought substantially higher conversion efficiency than was possible with any existing or proposed central-station electric generating plants. Cogeneration, which offered the possibility of increasing the role of electricity without the extremely high inefficiency penalties associated with central stations, has been increasingly researched and developed since those early experimental periods.

Many of the alternative systems developed since the 1970's--fuel cells, for example--were found to be particularly adaptable to dispersion. Bio-conversion offered a potential for energy from municipal wastes, agricultural residues, and terrestrial and marine energy farming. These technologies showed a high potential for producing methane gas suitable for driving cogeneration systems. The basically conservative technologists of the 1970's were followed by a more flexible group of energy specialists trained in a nondisciplinary or multidisciplinary context and able to innovate more freely.

The private sector has lowered winter thermostats, reduced hot water temperatures, used less hot water, raised air-conditioning thermostats, turned off unnecessary lights, and installed regulators on water lines for baths and showers and nondissipative rheostats on interior lighting.

The temperature of each room is independently controlled; only part of
each house is heated in winter; windows are controlled to accept, hold,
or reject solar and other heat as appropriate; high-efficiency window
air conditioners replace central units.

A number of these simple changes to which people readily adapted
were facilitated by restructuring utility rates, eliminating master
meters in multitenant buildings, giving discounts for energy efficiency,
charging peak-load prices, and promoting off-peak consumption patterns.
In addition, building codes were changed to emphasize energy savings,
and low-interest retrofit loans were offered for older houses.

Americans in general are now using less processed food. People
shop more frequently for fresh meat and produce, usually from the mobile
groceries that pass through neighborhoods daily. Frequent shopping
means less refrigeration, less spoilage and waste, and more sociability
in the neighborhood. For other shopping, small groceries and shops in
neighborhoods mean that less transportation is needed for shopping. Some
luxury food shops provide delivery service in response to call-in shopping lists.

Higher voltage electric transmission lines (240-360 V) for ranges
are increasing in popularity because these lines lose less energy. All
consumers have automatic pilot starters that ignite gas stoves or water
heaters when needed. Dishwashers are still used, except that now the
dishes dry without a heated drying cycle.

For the residential sector, total energy use in 2010 is 8.6 quads.
Air conditioning now accounts for 0.09 quad; space heating consumes 1.62
quads in older homes and 1.03 quads in newer homes; appliances have
increased their general efficiency by 40 percent since the 1970's and
now consume 0.53 quad; other miscellaneous uses account for 0.59 quad.

Commercial

The commercial sector has reduced its energy use since 1972 from 8.7 to
5.8 quads, or 67 percent of the previous total, even though output from
the sector has expanded. Most of this change has been the result of
less energy-intensive indoor climates.

As a general rule, bulk goods and services are moved to people,
rather than people to goods. These overall figures are an average;
there are regional variations in climate, fuel resources, types of construction, and conservation incentives.

Commerce has expanded dramatically in the overall number of commercial operations. There has been a gradual reversal of the pre-1975
trend as self-employed persons in this country shifted from 8 percent
of the labor force in 1970 to 30 percent of the labor force in 2010.
Approximately 84 million persons are self-employed in small farms, services, crafts, repair, and other businesses; about 65 percent of the
employed people are affiliated with these commercial endeavors, as workers, distributors, and so on.

As some businesses were decentralized, heat as a by-product from
generators began to be recycled to supplement building (and in some cases

community) heating needs, especially in the colder climates; the net saving in 2010 in such systems, relative to separate production of heat, is 25 percent. This space-heating saving is increased to 30 percent in one-half of the commercial buildings through shared heating and cooling units, increased insulation, and retrofitting; sharing units also reduces external wall exposure and heat-transfer losses. Double-entry doors are popular. Locating new buildings in relation to the sun and shade orientation allows maximum savings from internal and structural changes; this is particularly true in the colder climates of the Rockies and the Northeast, where the United States adopted the technique of optimizing outside area in volume to minimize heating needs. Total saving here was 10 percent for buildings thus situated (Bligh and Hamburger, 1973). Fuel-purchase permit regulations forced quicker design and construction changes in colder areas.

There are now lower illumination standards and wider use of low-power lighting to replace much of the former incandescent lighting. Metered space and water heating in commercial buildings and coin-timer-operated water heaters and outside illumination permit a total saving of 20 percent.

By using demand-at-point-of-use water heaters, as Europe and Japan have done for some time and as was done in the United States before World War II, the commercial sector is avoiding water-storage problems, pipe cool-down heat loss, and unnecessary use of hot water. New structures and use of solar energy for all water heating in some buildings, supplemented by recycled generator heat when necessary, allow for a large saving in hot-water heating in the commercial sector as a whole.

Transportation

Transportation systems, stimulated by strong action of the reorganized transportation unions, are more diversified in 2010. Although there has been a shift away from heavy to light trucks, some owner-operated, for transportation with cities and towns, some heavy trucks are still used for longer hauls. Contrary to former practice, trucks are used at near capacity; they travel in both directions with goods, not just one way with an empty return trip. Electric railway systems transport much of the industrial and commercial goods between major urban centers. Only 50 percent of the energy used in 1975 is needed for intracity transport of goods and produce; the transition to diesel fuel has accounted for 20 percent of this saving.

Use of energy in the entire transportation sector has been reduced from the 1972 level of 16.5 quads to 11.5 quads by 2010. Small, light, more efficient vehicles with greatly improved fuel economy and longer lasting parts have been introduced, and the per-capita number of miles traveled has been cut back.

Intercity passenger transport for trips up to 1000 miles is largely by rail. This shift has cut down air passenger transportation. Airline travel, however, requires less energy than before because of improved efficiencies in aircraft payloads due to the use of hydrogen fuel

(Bockris, 1975) and improved scheduling and operations (fewer flights carrying less extra fuel and flying at optimum altitudes).

Private automobiles are more efficient. Only about 25 percent of the short intercity trips are made in private cars, and many of these are carpool trips. The total energy consumption for distances under 10 miles is only 10 percent of what it was in 1970 (See Transportation Resource Group, 1976).

Advanced engine systems, such as the Sterling and Brayton cycles, have been developed and are in mass production. High-temperature alloys permit increases in combustion temperatures and accordingly in overall conversion efficiency. Composite materials are used for body structures, simultaneously decreasing weight and increasing safety.

Electric vehicles are common for short-range urban transport. Mini-bus transporters within the city, which criss-cross all parts of town, are widely used. Shifts in urban design to emphasize dense cores and high population densities along mass-transit corridors have had the direct effect of decreasing the vehicle miles traveled by 14 or 15 percent. In addition, there has been a reduction in the energy required to construct buildings and roads, supply services, and generally to fabricate and operate the transportation infrastructure.

The direct impact of urban mass-transit shifts on energy use is relatively small, but the impact on the associated infrastructure is large. The urban transit system of the 1970's exhibited large variations in direct-energy requirement—from 2000 Btu/passenger mile in Chicago to 4500 Btu/passenger mile in Albuquerque. Load factors on all systems are now higher.

Intercity high-speed transit for distances up to 500 miles is by ground. Magnetic levitation using superconducting magnets was explored by several nations, notably Japan, during the 1970's. The United States, which had dropped such small-scale programs at one time, reactivated its research to develop this technology.[a] An efficiency for goods transport equivalent to that which existed in Sweden in the 1970's led to a drop of 25 percent in the United States per-capita energy use for goods transport.

These combined savings leave consumption at 2.8 quads for automobiles, 2.2 quads for air travel (1.5 times the activity per capita of the 1970's), and 4.2 quads for truck transport, with no growth in per-capita activity. Miscellaneous uses remain at 1.7 quads. (See 72-quad scenario in chapter 5). This results in a total energy use of 10.7 quads.[b]

Industry

Industrial energy use amounts to around 27 quads, compared with 31 quads in the 1970's. Direct fuel and electricity usage has leveled off at

---

[a]It is important to perform energy analyses on all technologies before implementing them.

[b]Saving factors and per-capita activity assumptions in Table 32 have been changed as indicated; other factors are held constant.

about 17,000 kWh per capita in this sector, compared with 23,000 kWh per capita in the early 1970's.[a]

Good housekeeping measures alone now save 8 quads annually compared with 1972 energy use. Once energy conservation was accepted as a matter of policy in medium- and large-scale industry, the payoff in savings was worth the effort and initial capital investment. In the 1970's Raytheon and Lockheed demonstrated that fuel costs could be cut 23-30 percent through efficient engineering and sensible housekeeping. Dupont not only reduced fuel and energy consumption in existing plants but was among the first to promote the notion that extra initial capital outlays for fuel economy would be repaid many times over as companies recovered their total capital and operating costs over the life cycles of their plants and equipment.

Some of the earlier conservation measures that proved most effective were good housekeeping (5-6 quads less than 1972 fuel usage), steam/electric cogeneration for 50 percent of industrial process steam (4 quads), fuel conversion to direct-heat applications (0.75 quad), electricity from bottom cycling in 50 percent of direct-heat applications (0.5 quad), recycling of aluminum, iron, steel, and organic waste in urban refuse (1 quad), reduced throughput at oil refineries (1 quad), and reduced field and transport losses in natural-gas systems (1 quad) (Ross and Williams, 1977). (See Table 22.)

Encouraged by the Dow study (Dow Chemical, 1975), other firms discovered that cogeneration would provide 238 billion kWh of electricity to sell to electric utilities. Utilities in turn sold steam to industry. This saving reduced total utility investment between 1975 and 1985 by $29 billion for a national net saving of $16 billion (1975 dollars). Industries that cogenerated electricity earned a pretax rate of return of 20 percent on such investment (Dow Chemical, 1975).

Developments in energy conservation since the 1970's have combined to produce substantial cumulative savings. For example, cogenerated process heat (4.8 quads) has contributed significantly to industrial conservation (National Research Council, 1979).

Compared with industrial fuel and power use of 1972, the energy needs for certain industries, in quads, have remained nearly constant: aluminum (0.5 quad), glass (0.30), cement (0.5), construction (0.9), and food processing (1.5). Those for chemicals have risen from 4.7 to 5 quads (including feedstocks), those for petroleum have risen slightly from 3.3 to 3.5 quads, and those for steel have risen from 3 to 3.5 quads. Including an overall saving of 30 percent in energy intensity in other industrial processes (Berg, 1974), the total direct-energy-use figure is 25 quads. This figure excludes solar and other renewable energy sources for process heat, and electric generation losses; the solar capacity for process heat in a high-output future was estimated in the 1970's to be 48 quads. If only 25 percent of this estimated potential had been realized by 2010, a 40-quad society might have been realized. In this scenario 51 quads are from nonrenewable sources and 1 to 3 quads are from renewable sources.

---

[a]This is an extrapolation from the 1972 figures in Schipper and Lichtenberg (1976), p. 1001.

Methods for the direct use of coal on a small scale were revived
in the 1970's. The technologies under investigation then called for
massive units to burn coal for electricity generation, coal gasification,
and large industrial processes. Work in England suggested that small-
scale coal use was possible and environmentally acceptable. Modest-sized
fluidized bed burners were found to be technologically feasible. The
challenge is still to develop coal-handling equipment that is as easy to
use and as clean and reliable as oil- and gas-handling systems.

Agriculture

Farms are generally small, ranging from 60 to 5,000 acres, although some
large farms (over 5,000 acres) have expanded, and large farming machinery
is still used. Social custom, law, and the lack of large-scale long-
distance transport facilities keep most farms from growing inordinately
large.

Industrialized agricultural machinery is lighter and more efficient,
and new technologies have made most heavy machinery easier to use. Mini-
aturization has made it possible for both larger and smaller farms to
replace heavy equipment easily and efficiently, although many smaller
farms generally prefer to substitute a combination of lighter equipment
and slightly more labor-intensive methods.

Some energy is saved by changes in agricultural methods. Crops
grown in a given area are diversified so that plowing, cultivating, and
harvesting times are staggered. The same acreage is under cultivation
as in the 1970's, but fewer farm machines are needed to tend the crops.
The saving has been in energy used to produce the machinery, not in
energy used to run it. Small garden tractors are used on smaller acre-
ages, as was done for a number of years in Europe and Japan, because of
the scarcity of land and high population density in those areas (Ross
and Williams, 1977). All these factors combine to make farming considerably less fuel intensive than it used to be, even with the increase
in absolute numbers of farms.

More produce and livestock from local sources is being consumed
than in the past; some food is shipped by air, truck, or rail to more
distant locations. A good proportion of green produce from California,
Florida, and other "sunshine" states is still shipped to other locations
with less favorable climates, and Maine lobsters are still found in
Dallas restaurants.

One of the long-range by-products of decreased energy use per capita
has been the ability to deal with drought conditions throughout the
United States. New crop varieties and watering methods that require
less water have been introduced. There are now extensive national coop-
erative land banks, so that farmers are able to follow the rain to a
greater degree than in the 1970's. Drought areas are put into forage
or dedicated to light grazing while many farmers move temporarily to
areas of heavier-than-normal rainfall. The use of chemical fertilizers
and pesticides is much reduced because of symbiotic fixation of nitrogen
and biological control of pests.

DISCUSSION

Values influence all decision making, even those that seem most objective.
We live in a culture, however, in which we rarely dare to admit that
judgments are value-laden. It is because we place high value on rationality and objectivity that we find ourselves enamored of numbers and
eager to locate the scientific or economically rational reasons for policy. In fact, however, when uncertainties are high, most decisions are
probably value judgments cloaked with rational and scientific facts
(Colson, 1973).

One might suppose that raising the price of energy might reduce
energy consumption or that increased prices would stimulate production of
more sources of energy. But adopting these options only exacerbates the
problem: escalating the price of energy may reduce the consumption of
energy somewhat (albeit at greater cost to some than to others) but may
well increase the generation of energy from even less healthful sources.

In the 53-quad scenario the actors--consumers and decision makers--
become _aware_ that there are alternatives to "more is better" at any cost.
This process is indeed coming about through massive information in the
arts of economical crop production, heating, driving, construction, and
manufacturing. Thus we are getting to the point at which the consumers
and decision makers are aware of a far greater number of choices than
before. It is as though blinders have been taken from our vision and
many equally exciting and perhaps healthier paths of action have opened
before us. As our values change, so may our criteria for decision making.
It is the hierarchy of cultural values that determines in what spheres
of life people apply their price-based economizing and in what others
they exercise virtues such as generosity, reciprocity, and altruism
(Cancian, 1966).

Our diet, for example, is such a sphere--with increasing cultural
emphasis on bodily health and slimness, overeaters are in fact considered
almost sick in this society: they go to dieticians and doctors to have
their correct choices made clear, and to their mirrors, their friends,
and Weight Watchers for social approval or disapproval.

Similarly, even with our current consumption patterns, we may want
to consider how the social body can best be served. Already more economical autos from abroad, home-grown foods, and the recycling of waste
materials are subjects of prestige and approval among certain classes,
even when they are not rewarded by cost savings. The American people
are no less able to respond to a rearranged hierarchy of values than are
the other peoples of the world. We might almost claim that, having been
the recipients of plenty, and having lived through the most open economy
in history, the American people are in a better position to evaluate
their system and to make rational choices from the hierarchy of personal
and national values than other peoples who are still striving for freedom
and plenty.

In the 1970's, the energy industry used a disproportionate amount of
the country's investment capital relative to its sales and its low labor
use. In this scenario we note that, as conservation policies were implemented, energy-industry expenditures slowed, saving capital, reducing

pressure on interest rates, and permitting more personal consumption of goods and services and investment elsewhere. Planners learned that capital requirements for saving energy were often less than for building the equivalent capacity for generating energy. A study by the American Institute of Architects (1974), for example, showed that retrofitting older buildings or constructing new energy-efficient buildings could save the equivalent of 12 million barrels of oil per day by 1990, "about as much energy as the projected 1990 production capacity of any one of the prime energy systems: domestic oil, nuclear energy, domestic and imported natural gas, or coal." The theory and practice of a waste-free economy gradually demystified the spurious assumption that energy growth was equal to economic growth.

The question remains: How quickly can such value shifts occur in society? We have on record major lifestyle changes that are results of new technology (such as the automobile and air transportation), of new religions, of crises such as drought or famine, or of unconscious value changes, such as those relating to human fertility or to drug use. It is also possible to bring about change through a new morality. In the 53-quad society, the shift in values is motivated by a variety of pressures, which are the ultimate consequence of terminal hypertrophy.

Life has changed since 1900 and will continue to change until 2010 and beyond, no matter what our energy policy. The century has brought, among other things, credit buying; a greater cost of government; increased home ownership; a stronger labor movement; shorter work hours; increased reliance on drugs; more entertainment in the home by means of radio, phonograph, and television; increased communication by telephone and other electronic means; migration from farm to cities, and now to the suburbs and smaller cities and towns; age-segregated neighborhoods; a revolution in sexual mores; a shift from thrift to a throwaway style of living and the beginnings of a shift back again; the civil rights movement; decreased family size from factors both related and unrelated to fertility; and a larger proportion of college-educated people.

Massive planned change is a recent phenomenon, and there is a literature that attempts to isolate degrees of cultural persistence or change in the face of such plans. The direction of change--top-down or bottom-up--is one important factor in rate of change and may also be an indicator of success. The study of planned social change has shown that change implemented from the top down tends to fail when the top does not understand the values and conditions of the target population (Massell, 1968). The War on Poverty was such a failure. Any plans for implementing an energy policy should be cognizant of the literature on success and failure of planned change in a democratic setting. In this scenario, the instrument for change was a closing of the gaps among government, industry, and citizens in the planning process.

APPENDIX: NOTES TO TABLE 32

Saving factors as in Table 22, unless otherwise noted.

1. For existing housing stock that will not be replaced, see Chapter 4. The same figures are used here.

2. For new and replacement stock of housing, the method used to calculate the energy figure for space heating was as follows:

Major assumption: 50 percent of housing built will be multiunit. This yields a stock of housing in 2010 that is 43 percent multiunit:

Type	Btus/unit in 1976	Units built (millions)	Btus in 1976 efficiency (10^{15})
Single unit	1.5×10^8	21.1	3.165
Multiunit	6×10^8	29.6	1.776
Mobile	1.0×10^8	3.17	0.317
Total			5.258 quads

Multiplied by saving factor $(1 - 0.72)$ .28

1.47 quads (without solar)

Major assumption: 10 million units solar (5 million single-unit and 5 million multiunit):

Single unit: $1.5 \times 10^8 \times 5 \times 10^6 \; = \; 0.75 \times 10^{15}$

Multiunit: $0.6 \times 10^8 \times 5 \times 10^6 \; = \; 0.30 \times 10^{15}$

Total   1.05 quads

If solar is factored in, $(5.258 - 1.05) = 4.208 \times 0.28 = 1.18$ quads (with solar).

District heat assumption: 10 percent of single units and 25 percent of multiunits (20-percent saving).

Single unit: $1.5 \times 10^8 \times 2.11 \times 10^6 \; = \; 0.3165 \times 10^{15}$

Multiunit: $0.6 \times 10^8 \times 7.4 \times 10^6 \; = \; 0.444 \times 10^{15}$

Total $0.7605 \times 0.2 \; =$

0.152 quad saving

Total for new housing = 1.18 - 0.152 = 1.03 quad with solar and district heating. Note: With district heating, electricity is also generated at a rate of 0.5 units per heat unit. The 0.76 quad electricity generated by district heat is subtracted from electric generation losses for the residential sector.

3. As in the 72-quad scenario, with a slightly lower saving factor because there are fewer units in new homes.

4. As in 72-quad scenario.

5. As in 72-quad scenario.

6. No per-capita growth because no per-capita GNP growth. Saving factor, 40 percent.

7. No per-capita growth because no per-capita GNP growth. Saving factor, 40 percent.

8. Assumes: Driving-age population in 2010 = 202.43 million; 0.6 vehicles per driver = 0.44 vehicles per capita, 6550 miles per vehicle (0.75% per year decrease); number of vehicles in 2010 = 121.46 million; vehicle miles = 795.55 billion, fleet average mileage = 35 mpg, gallons of gasoline consumed = 22.730 x 10^9 (1 gallon = 1.25 x 10^5 Btu). Total energy use, 2.84 quads.

9. For air, assumes increased activity per capita of 1.5, no growth, and reduced demand for business travel (with substitution of telecommunications for travel). Increase in air traffic limited to this amount. Saving factor is 50 percent, as in 72-quad scenario.

10. Increased use of trucks for short-haul deliveries offset by shift from truck to rail for longer distances. Activity per capita remains the same with different composition. Saving factor is 15 percent as in 72-quad scenario.

11. Other: mostly bus and rail. Some increase with shift from truck. Pipeline use reduced somewhat.

12. Electrical generation losses calculated as in 72-quad scenario assuming the same distribution of electrical consumption by sector as there. Slight reduction in residential sector because of cogeneration from district heating (see note 2).

13. Commercial: Slight reduction in energy intensity per square meter compared with that in Table 22, but this is offset by an increase in per-capita activity of about 10 percent to account for the slight shift from manufacturing toward service.

14. Industry: Although the Demand and Conservation Panel (1976) thinks
    that a 40-percent saving is possible, it presupposes a growth rate
    that will enable industries to retire old plants and equipment and
    replace them with more efficient ones. Since we are assuming no
    per-capita growth, it is unlikely that the full saving potential
    will be realized. Here we have reduced the saving to 30 percent.
    Because of the assumed increase in services, industrial consumption
    per capita is reduced slightly. Reduction of losses in energy pro-
    cessing is offset by synfuels.

15. Industrial generation losses calculated at 90 percent of the losses
    in the 72-quad scenario. This is an overestimate, ignoring sales
    of waste heat to housing clusters.

REFERENCES

American Institute of Architects. 1974. A Nation of Energy-Efficient Buildings by 1990. Washington, D.C.: American Institute of Architects.

Berg, C. 1974. Conservation in Industry. Science 184:4134.

Berton, P. 1969. The Smug Minority. New York: Doubleday.

Best, A., and A. Andreasen. 1977. Consumer Response to Unsatisfactory Purchases: A Survey of Perceived Defects, Voicing Complaints and Obtaining Redress. Law and Society Review 11:701-742.

Bligh, T. P., and R. Hamburger. 1973. Conservation of Energy by Use of Underground Space. In Legal, Economical, and Energy Considerations in the Use of Underground Space. Washington, D.C.: National Science Foundation (NSF/RA/S 74-002).

Bockris, J. 1975. Energy: The Solar-Hydrogen Alternative. New York: Halsted Press and John Wiley.

Boulding, K. 1949-1950. Inccme or Welfare. Review of Economic Studies 17(2):77-86.

Callenbach, E. 1972. Living Poor with Style. New York: Bantam Books.

Cancian, F. 1966. Maximization as Norm, Strategy, and Theory. American Anthropologist 68:465-470.

Colson, E. 1973. Tranquility for the Decision-Maker. In Cultural Illness and Health (Anthropological Studies No. 9). Washington, D.C.: American Anthropological Association.

Demand and Conservation Panel. 1976. Draft report to the Committee on Nuclear and Alternative Energy Systems, National Research Council, Washington, D.C. December.

Dow Chemical Company. 1975. Industrial Energy Center. Report prepared for the National Science Foundation. June.

Linder, S. B. 1970. The Harried Leisure Class. New York: Columbia University Press.

Massell, G. J. 1968. Law as an Instrument of Revolutionary Change in a Traditional Milieu. Law and Society Review 2:179-228.

National Research Council. 1979. Domestic Potential of Solar and Other Renewable Energy Sources. Solar Resource Group, Supply and Delivery Panel, Committee on Nuclear and Alternative Energy Systems. Supporting Paper 6. Washington, D.C.: National Academy of Sciences.

Pilati, D. 1976. Building Energy Use Scenarios, 1976-2010. 1976. Paper prepared for Demand and Conservation Panel, Committee on Nuclear and Alternative Energy Systems, National Research Council, Washington, D.C.

Ross, M., and R. Williams. 1977. The Potential for Fuel Conservation. Technology Review 79(4):48-57.

Schipper, L., and A. L. Lichtenberg. 1976. Efficient Energy Use and Well Being: The Swedish Example. Science 194:1001-1013.

Scitovsky, T. 1976. The Joyless Economy. New York: Oxford University Press.

Stanford Research Institute. 1975. Comparison of Energy Consumption between West Germany and the United States. Menlo Park, Calif.: Stanford Research Institute.

Transportation Resource Group. 1976. Draft report to the Demand and Conservation Panel, Committee on Nuclear and Alternative Energy Systems, National Research Council, Washington, D.C.

Wall Street Journal. 1976. Dropouts Revisited . . . Men Who Left Work to Seek Happiness. December 27.

7   WHO SHALL DECIDE?

Experts are people. We know little about our scientists, our technologists, and those who are elected or appointed to make our policies. We
need to be informed about their professional training, their perspectives on the world, the structures of their work places, and the
unexpressed values by which they judge and select their goals. These
constraints within which experts function must be made a part of our
understanding so that we can evaluate their advice with an eye to their
stakes in the outcome.

Expertise is associated with objectivity. But what may be functional to the advancement of the individual and his profession may come
to be inappropriate for social problem solving. Then, too, the thinking,
the logic, and the conclusions of experts include hidden value judgments
that either lie beyond their fields of expertise or are not shared by
their peers or by the society for which they purport to speak. The
problems in energy are both technical and nontechnical. The latter
aspects have been ignored, or, worse, preempted in the technical
expert's analyses, often without the knowledge of the nontechnician.

A major source of distrust of experts is that most of the facts
about the energy situation are highly technical. People are under-
standably uncomfortable about having to make long-range, crucially
important policy decisions on the basis of information they find difficult to comprehend. They must therefore turn to experts for explanations
and guidance through the tangle of technologies. But the experts seem
to be identified with the very industries which stand to profit most by
the nation's continuing along the traditional high-growth energy path.
Such experts assure us that technology will, in time, solve most, if not
all, of the problems now confronting us as the energy crisis.

Additionally, technological forecasts, like predictions in every area of human life, can be mistaken. Experts can be wrong about how soon a technology will become available:

"As far as sinking a ship with a bomb is concerned, you just can't do it."

Rear Admiral Clark Woodward, 1939

They can be wrong about the uses to which the technological innovation will be put:

"(Airplanes) will eventually be fast, they will be used in sport, but they are not to be thought of as commercial carriers. To say nothing of the danger, the sizes must remain small and the passengers few, because the weight will, for the same design, increase as the cube of the dimensions, while the supporting surfaces will only increase as the square."

Octave Chanute, American aviation pioneer, 1904

And they can be wrong about the invention's consequences for technology itself:

"...Even if the (screw) propeller had the power of propelling a...vessel, it would be found altogether useless in practice, because the power being applied in the stern it would be absolutely impossible to make the vessel steer."

Sir William Symonds, Surveyor of the British Navy, 1837

If, therefore, experts display themselves to be as fallible as the rest of us within their own areas of expertise, some persons have begun to ask for their credentials for claiming our unquestioning assent when they move outside their fields and begin to forecast social and cultural consequences of the technologies they purvey. Even if we were to grant (and there is little reason for doing so) that they may know better than we how likely such consequences are, they are not thereby in a better position than we to say how desirable they are.

Expertise is associated with decision making within narrow confines. With increased specialization comes an isolation that separates the expert from the lay person, and the expert in one field from the expert in another. Such isolation and its accompanying homogeneity may result in productivity for the individual and the profession while at the same time decreasing human benefits generally. The anthropologist A. L. Kroeber (1948) summarized this situation without commenting on the pitfalls:

> As the total culture is thereby varied and enriched, it
> also becomes more difficult for each member of the society
> really to participate in most of its activities. He begins
> to be an onlooker at most of it, then a by-stander, and
> may end up with indifference to the welfare of his society
> and the values of his culture. He falls back upon the
> immediate problems of his livelihood and the narrowing
> range of enjoyments still open to him, because he senses
> that his society and his culture have become indifferent
> to him.

The problems of late-twentieth-century America have a seamless quality about them that does not recognize the well-delineated spheres of expertise.

The ideology of the marketplace is one cluster of values that permeates the way experts tend to think about sociopolitical problems in our country. In the theory of market ideology, individuals and organizations make market decisions, and these all somehow add up (with the aid of Adam Smith's "invisible hand") to satisfactory choices for the society as a whole. We recognize the efficiency of the market as a superb mechanism for ordering this immensely complex process. What usually goes unnoticed, however, is the important though subtle role of the culture in guiding the process.

It is not necessarily true that private self-interest alone, operating in the marketplace, results in wise social choices. The culture that guides the microdecisions determines the kinds of social macrodecisions that result. If, for example, the culture has negligible concern for future generations, then the market alone will permit, even encourage, depletion of nonrenewable resources and spoliation of the environment, talk of "internalizing the externalities" notwithstanding. The future will be discounted at rates that profit the present generation. If the culture contains no ethic of protecting the poor and the weak, whether persons or nations, then market decision making will make the powerful richer and the weak poorer.

Paul Diesing (1962) distinguishes five kinds of rationality that operate in modern societies: technological, economic, social, legal, and political. He describes how economic rationality has gradually been gaining dominance over social and political choices:

> Most of the sociocultural changes occurring in the Western
> world in recent centuries are either a part of, or a result
> of, economic and technological progress. One cultural element
> after another has been absorbed into the ever-widening
> economy, subjected to the test of economic rationality,
> rationalized, and turned into a commodity or factor of pro-
> duction. So pervasive has this process been that it now
> seems that anything can be thought of as a commodity and
> its value measured by a price...time, land, capital, labor,
> also personality itself, ...art objects, ideas, experiences,

enjoyment itself, and even social relations. As these
become commodities they are all subject to a process of
moral neutralization.

Our society's decisions are now based on neat and quantified but limited
economic rationality. Economic goals have been substituted for social
goals; what are properly means--technology and the economy--have been
elevated to the rank of ends.

The economist Kenneth Boulding (1969) has distinguished between
economic decisions, appropriately made with the aid of economic rationality, and "heroic" decisions, which must be made another way. Whether
the United States should give overwhelming support to developing solar
energy and to husbanding nonrenewable resources would seem to call for
such a heroic decision. One of the chief architects of our present
political system, Edmund Burke (quoted 1975), would have argued so from
his view of the social contract with the yet unborn:

> Society is indeed a contract...[but] as the ends of such a
> partnership cannot be obtained in many generations, it be-
> comes a partnership not only between those who are living,
> but between those who are living, those who are dead, and
> those who are to be born.

To the extent, therefore, that experts are influenced by the marketplace in their sociotechnical advice, we must hold back from
embracing their views wholeheartedly, for values beyond the marketplace
will figure heavily in public acceptance of a national energy policy.

There are lifestyle issues and judgments that the marketplace alone
will not settle. For example, more single family dwellings, urged on
by mortgage policies that implicitly value economic development more
than environmental preservation, mean more strip mines and greater
pressure to build large-scale and more polluting energy parks. How do
we balance these two conflicting tendencies, one that apparently im-
proves our well-being, the other that reduces it, both of them hard to
measure? Clearly, the marketplace and the technical fixes will do much
to alleviate many of the difficulties. At issue to energy planners,
however, is the risk that the marketplace will not do enough, or that
the marketplace will not function, or that political interests will
influence short-term market signals so that our economic structure will
not truly respond to the beneficial signals that the marketplace might
offer.

In the chapters describing the 72- and 53-quad societies, we emphasized two factors that enter into the per-capita demand for energy:
(1) the various goods and services consumers demand and (2) the energy
intensity of producing each of those goods and services. We noted that
the most important strategies for reducing energy demand would be to
reduce these intensities by substituting other resources for energy. We
noted also that, because different activities have different intrinsic
energy intensities, changes in choice of activities can influence energy
demands. In the 53- and 72-quad scenarios, we suggested variations in

the running of households, the stringing together of auto trips, and variations in the size of homes and the total miles driven. These structural or lifestyle factors, although influenced by energy concerns, such as costs and pollution, seem to be driven by forces larger than energy-related market considerations. For although the growth of suburbs and the increased travel suburbanites needed to obtain services were certainly facilitated by the availability of inexpensive gasoline, mortgage and land-use policies quite unrelated to energy concerns were also important factors. This is not to say that decisions to subsidize suburbanization and single family dwellings were incorrect but only that they were made on the basis of individualistic values, perhaps to the exclusion of micro- and macro-economic considerations.

We need not ban large cars or limit the distances car owners may travel. But we may want to redefine the marketplace upon which we have heaped many of our social goals through subsidies, taxes, rules, and propaganda in the form of advertising. Choices that may be rational in the personal sense may conflict with social or macro-economic goals. For example, most people feel little urgency to buy smaller cars or to drive less. Such reasons as national security, or that such actions would reduce the demand and price of gasoline to users, or that environmental damage from both the harvesting and use of gasoline would be reduced, or that the future price of energy to yet-unborn or inactive participants in economic or social decisions would be lower, have weighed little with them so far. Such concerns are difficult to express in theory in the marketplace, especially when they involve activities rather than intensities. Technology can fix the amounts of energy required to produce at least some goods and services. It cannot fix changes in the activities people undertake.

The pressure to continue to subsidize energy development rather than energy efficiency is today juxtaposed with pressure to control energy prices. Consumer groups are supporting energy-price controls, not to gain artificially low energy prices (cheap energy) but to prevent the artificially high energy prices that would occur in the absence of controls as domestic energy producers raise their prices to the OPEC cartel's monopoly price. The result would be distortion of the entire economy and inequitable transfers of wealth, as is true of all monopoly pricing. The value judgment has been made, however, that cheap energy is good and that society should be structured around cheap energy as long as possible.

It is certain that the increase in the number of homes after World War II influenced energy demands. That energy appeared in copious quantities at low prices, however, suggests that in the short range the wisdom of this sprawl, viewed from the standpoint of energy or other resource use, did not require questioning. Today, of course, we are paying the price of our negligent approach to resources in pollution, high-marginal-cost replacements for petroleum, and land-use patterns that impede transition to less energy-intensive transportation. Virtually all our energy options, except for most forms of solar energy, involve substantial environmental dangers, but in our hurry to produce rather than save energy, we find ourselves pressured by many interest

groups to make such judgments about trade-offs as: How much is present
consumption at a low price worth in terms of environmental costs and
risks? The implication is that we can keep our costs low by passing
them on to the future, the ecosystem, and so on.

In summary, political and social decisions about resource use
extend beyond the marketplace and are influenced by subjective values
and judgments. This is not improper in itself. What is alarming is
that experts often pretend to be able to perform objective analyses on
energy systems or energy users because they are unwilling to acknowledge
the values on which their decisions or analyses are made. But we cannot
permit experts to decide which energy system we shall have if they use
only the vantage points of technology and economics.

It is imperative that our long-range energy planning be integrated
with other kinds of planning and that all long-range aspects of the
energy problem, especially environmental costs, be integrated with more
traditional marketplace factors, no matter how difficult they may be to
quantify.

Our worry, however, is whether we take into consideration the problems and risks associated with energy use in our policy deliberations
and in our choices of lifestyle. The Energy Research and Development
Administration (1976) spoke of developing energy resources in ways that
will not restrict lifestyle choices because of energy availability--but
the direct and indirect costs associated with making increasingly larger
amounts of various energy forms available will themselves restrict lifestyle choices to some degree, because rising costs will fall dispropor-
tionately on the poor, because the environmental values that are dear
to some groups may be sacrificed in the interests of higher energy production for the nation as a whole, and because centralized decision
making appears to be a necessary concomitant of any high-energy future.

Centralized decision making takes the form of government decrees,
expropriation of land, massive use of tax funds, and government support
for the social infrastructures required to attract and support large
numbers of people who harvest new oil, coal, gas, geothermal, solar,
and uranium supplies, as we are currently seeing in the investigation
into the costs of the Alaskan pipeline.

To what extent do we want to influence our ways of life--and
thereby our energy demands--to reduce these residuals? This is an
extremely serious question, and the answer may lie for the most part
outside the marketplace. We would argue that planners need to incorporate more information than cents-per-kilowatt-hour in the bottom lines
of their calculations.

REFERENCES

Boulding, K. 1969. Economics as a Moral Science. American Economic
Review 59(1):1-12.

Burke, E. 1975. Quoted in entry on Conservatism. Encyclopedia
Britannica, 15th ed., vol. 5:62-69.

Diesing, P. 1962. Reason in Society. Urbana, Ill.: University of
Illinois Press. p. 5.

Energy Research and Development Administration. 1976. A National Plan
for Energy Research, Development, and Demonstration: Creating Energy
Choices for the Future. Washington, D.C.: U.S. Government Printing
Office (ERDA-76-1).

Kroeber, A. L. 1948. Anthropology. New York: Harcourt, Brace.
p. 291.